THE POWER OF

INFLUENCE

The new business agenda of the '90s focuses on working with change and developing people's potential and performance. The *People Skills for Professionals* series brings this empowering theme to life with a range of practical human resource guides for anyone who wants to get the best from their people in the world of the learning organisation.

THE POWER OF INFLUENCE

Intensive influencing skills in business

Tom E. Lambert

NICHOLAS BREALEY
PUBLISHING
LONDON

'Happily children are generally too inattentive to derive injury from learning.' Reading Without Tears

To the children of the Information Age, especially Carole and David

First published by
Nicholas Brealey Publishing Limited in 1996

21 Bloomsbury Way
London
WC1A 2TH

Box 905
Sonoma
California 95476

© Tom E. Lambert 1996
The rights of Tom E. Lambert to be identified as the author of this work have been
asserted in accordance with the Copyright, Designs and Patents Act 1988.

Library of Congress Cataloging in Publication Data applied for

ISBN 1-85788-116-8 (Hardback)
ISBN 1-85788-115-X (Paperback)

British Library Cataloguing in Publication Data
A catalogue record for this book is available from the British Library.

Contents

Introduction 1

Had I the time to write a book, I would make the human mind as plain as the road from Charing Cross to St. Pauls.

(James Mill)

To be persuasive we must be believable; to be believable we must be credible; to be credible we must be truthful.

(Edward R. Murrow)

I had no education – so I had to use my brains.

(Bill Shankly)

DOING THE WRONG THING IN THE RIGHT WAY

When I wrote my first business book, one critic, clearly disappointed, wrote: 'This is not an academic book.'

Few criticisms could have pleased me more. My intention had been to write a plain book for plain readers. This book is no different.

My goal is to write a comprehensive review of influence psychology, but most of all I want to write a useful book. I shall be dealing with areas of carefully validated research, but I shall make every effort to combine plain speaking with plain language.

When I conduct seminars I have a recurrent fear that people may leave looking highly satisfied and saying: 'That was interesting.' I know from long experience that 'interesting' is far removed from useful. I hope that people leave my seminars – and put down this book – with the thought: 'Now I know precisely what to do.'

But enough of my plans and wishes. The important person in the oddly intimate yet distant relationship between writer and reader is the reader. What do you want as you pick up and consider whether you should give some of your valuable time to reading this book?

I have no realistic alternative but to hope and guess. Guess, because although I can ask my question I cannot hear your answer, and hope because I am writing a book with a purpose.

WHAT THIS BOOK WILL DO FOR YOU

My aim is to enable readers to survive and prosper in a rapidly changing business and social environment. I will put before you a comprehensive guide to influence psychology so you may use ethical, non-manipulative and above all effective techniques of persuasion in your working, social and domestic life. I will also show you highly manipulative techniques of very doubtful moral worth and how they are used by those Cialdini calls the 'compliance professsionals'.

I provide the good and the bad and sometimes the ugly; the good as an authority toolkit for all those who must influence the behaviour of others, whether as managers, salespeople, parents or teachers; the bad as an innoculation against the insidious powers of those who are without conscience and whose wiles make us all the potential victims of conmen (and women) of every kind. A quick dip into the ugly, in this case the extremely ugly methods of religious cults, provides real world evidence of how the unsavoury use the unacceptable to promote their abominable ends.

THE IMPORTANCE OF INFLUENCE

We must not treat people as mere things to be manipulated, but as free beings, to be treated with respect as themselves.

(Immanuel Kant)

Social discourse between individuals and groups is replete with examples of one person seeking to influence another. It is almost impossible to imagine a society in which all communication is neutral. If I believe that something is in your interests I will go to almost any lengths to persuade you that you should do *this*, rather than *that*. And I know that if I fail to persuade you, someone else, possibly less concerned with your interests, will be quick to put in their two pennies worth.

Like it or not, in our society you must be prepared to influence the behaviour of others – not to do so is often simply an abdication of responsibility. If you are going to be a persuader you might as well be a good one, and to be good at something you need information.

For information about human behaviour logic suggests that you look at the science which is devoted to its study.

If you are skimming through this introduction in a bookshop, try this. Wander across to the Psychology shelves, pick up the most weighty text books and look up 'influence' and 'persuasion' in the indexes. I am prepared to bet that you will, at best, find a few niggardly pages devoted to these critical subject areas.

Does that mean that little is known about them? Far from it. It is not a question of ignorance, only of selection.

RAPID CHANGE

One of the more positive legacies of the Thatcher era has been a growing understanding of how quickly culture can be changed. In 13 short years not only did British society swing from caring pluralism to egocentric individualism, but under the influence of Mrs Thatcher and Mr Reagan much of the world, including Yeltsin's Russia, followed suit, with results which I will leave to the reader to evaluate. I regard the knowledge of how quickly social change can be created as positive rather than otherwise because the speed of cultural change in one direction suggests a capacity to make equally rapid changes in any desired direction. There is increasing evidence that genetic evolution is being replaced by cultural evolution. The genes are being overtaken by the memes (basic elements of communication).

If we want a better world we only need pick up the tools to

be well on the way to finishing the job. For the committed this book will provide some of the key tools.

Why are leading edge influencing skills needed today more than ever before in human history? Bear with me for a page or two while I explain, very briefly, under four distinct headings.

POSTMODERNISM AND A CHANGING WORLD

The first may seem trivial, but it is a fact of our postmodern world that technology, where it exists, will be used. In medicine, for example, CT scanners are routinely used to assure those who experience pain, discomfort or fear that there is 'nothing wrong' with them. Frequently such technological approaches are more in the interest of the doctor who wishes to use the current toy than they are helpful to the patient who needs the time and psychological space to express how they feel and what they experience. Thus use can lead to misuse and even abuse.

We understand the processes which can be applied to direct and manage human behaviour better than ever before. There is a persuasive argument that suggests that the smaller and therefore the more authoritative the group that has the techniques, the greater the potential for abuse. Thus there is a need for this technology to be widely understood.

There are, however, more immediate and obviously practical reasons.

THE CHANGING SITUATION OF MANAGEMENT

Expensive, time-consuming business initiatives such as business process reengineering, TQM and empowerment often fail dismally to give a return on the very considerable investment made when introducing them. Research in Germany, the United Kingdom and America suggest, for example, a failure rate for business process reengineering projects of between 76 and 80 per cent. Some empowerment initiatives lead to a frustrating combination of paralysis and anarchy, and if TQM is defined as 'consistently delighting the customer at minimum cost' the failure rate is very close to 100 per cent.

This does not indicate that business process reengineering, empowerment and the rest are a waste of corporate time – far from it. What it does is to draw our attention to the truism that if people are critical to the success of an initiative you must have the means to win their hearts as well as their minds. People do not always immediately recognise the future value of change. You need, in an early period of uncertainty, to be able to show them convincingly what is in it for them. Get them to share an attractive enough vision and they will bust a gut, if they must, to make it work. For that you need leading edge influencing skills. But it doesn't end there.

The growth of telecommuting and outsourcing of key services means that influence will in future need to be exercised at a distance, or managers and leaders will have no choice but to abdicate their responsibility and hope for the best in what may prove to be far from the best of all possible worlds. This too will demand something special in terms of influence.

A report published by the Institute of Management in May 1995 tells us that 76 per cent of managers surveyed reported low morale and supportiveness within their work teams following headcount reductions and redundancies. Add that to the Handy formula that we are now requiring from those at work three times the output with half the staff, and we have a a field in which leadership influence is going to need all the help that it can get. Charles Handy also tells us that business is, and will continue to be, increasingly dependent on highly skilled, independent-minded and potentially highly mobile *knowledge workers*. Getting to first base in terms of offering leadership to these new prima donnas of the commercial world will require exceptional persuasive skills and the cost of lacking the knowledge and ability to retain control can be high. The Nick Leeson affair at Barings Bank should be a salutory lesson to all who believe that specialists should be simply given their heads and left alone to ensure maximum performance.

A rapidly changing business world is still often in the grip of managerial dinosaurs. Managers who have new and valid ideas often have little chance of getting them accepted in the business Jurassic Park. Ideas will be accepted and implemented if, and probably only if, the thinkers acquire and use state of the art influencing techniques.

In today's and increasingly in tomorrow's business world, the salesperson must be perceived by the customer as an ally and a resource. This means that the salesperson will sell as much on the basis of their own status and reputation as on the intrinsic value of their service or product. They must, therefore, present themselves as totally ethical and totally professional. Many, if not all, will need to access a whole new level of skill and a range of highly effective customer-facing behaviours.

As products and services increasingly become globalised and standardised, more and more customers and clients seek a long-term relationship with the salesperson. Building such a relationship cannot be left to chance or chemistry – it demands considerable knowledge sensitively applied.

While costs of manufacture have reduced, the costs of marketing, sales and distribution have escalated. Future competitive advantage will be the result of low-cost referral business. Customer care and total quality programmes have invited the customer to anticipate higher value at lower cost. Referrals may prove to be the only way to make future cost savings, as process savings become more and more difficult to find and referrals come most readily to those who demonstrate the most subtle and sensitive skills.

In the insurance industry from 1 January 1995 there has been a legal requirement for commission disclosure. There is no reason to believe that increased regulation of selling will not be introduced into other areas. Experience in the insurance industry suggests that those able to apply effective techniques to build customer relationships have been able to take an assertive approach to disclosure and have gained a clear and considerable selling edge.

Many people who find themselves in a selling role today would not have regarded themselves as salespeople until circumstances dictated the need. People running small companies and one man bands, people who often have high levels of technical skill, find that they need to go out and knock on doors – and most are far from comfortable with the role. Those who seek training and experience the techniques offered by traditional 'pile 'em high, sell 'em cheap' programmes find the validity of what is offered and the ethics of its application equally doubtful. More people than ever need access to influencing techniques which are consistent with their values and which research and experience both support. Most of all the technically adept demand a structure, almost an algorithm, on which they can rely.

Closing the circle of argument, we all need an understanding of influence technology to recognise and resist the blandishments of the sound bite politician, the religious leader on a cosmic ego trip and the snake-oil charms of the 'compliance professional' – but is it merely as a form of innoculation against possible harm that all concerned and caring people need to understand the tools of influence? Or should each of us be prepared to go beyond understanding and learn to apply them?

BUT – SELLING
SKILLS FOR
CITIZENS?

Making your voice heard is not necessarily easy. It is easiest, however, for those who can bring to their community not just the desire to be heard, but the capability to put their message across persuasively. We all have a right to a vision of the future. Those who add to that vision the skill to make others share it have a chance of turning dream into reality. I have more to say on this in the brief epilogue to this book, but first and most importantly, whether you are a manager, salesperson or a concerned citizen, let us get to grips with the skills.

A WORD ABOUT THE BOOK

This is a practical, not an academic book. It is designed to combine maximum information with maximum practical value. It is based on a total of more than 130 years of research into influencing techniques in all parts of the world, with the information presented in a useable, 'how to' style. Jargon has been avoided where possible, but where technical terms are essential they are defined.

To enable readers to find their way easily to the areas they most need, the book moves from the practical to the more esoteric. This chapter has outlined the business and social background to the book. It explains *why* a change is desirable, and particularly *why now*. Chapter 2 begins a 'how to do it' guide, after which each chapter takes a key area of proven influence technology and discusses why it is important and how to use it. Having explained in detail *what* to do and *how* to do it, occasional chapters, for example Chapter 4, provide the research background which will enable you to understand why the method works and therefore apply it with confidence. Chapters 10 and 11 are a little more 'philosophical' and are designed to help thoughtful readers to enhance their own world view. The Appendix is intended to be like the notes which you might receive at the end of a high quality training seminar. These comprehensive and detailed notes summarise the action-centred content of the book and act as a quick reference for the busy professional.

SUMMARY

If you need to:

- manage and influence behaviour in a rapidly changing business environment
- sell products or services to ever more discriminating clients or customers
- persuade others to accept and implement your good ideas
- deal with difficult people, whether bosses, employees, customers, pupils or relatives
- avoid the snares of the slick salesperson intent on offloading their dubious merchandise regardless of your needs
- build ongoing relationships based on trust while getting others to do what you want
- find that influencing other people's behaviour becomes easier every time you do it

And if you want to do it in a professional way using sound psychological principles, but no cheap tricks, this book will tell you how.

Unprincipled Influencing   2

WHAT YOU WILL GAIN FROM THIS CHAPTER
● An understanding of how we are hardwired by our evolutionary history to be susceptible to specific influencing factors ● What those factors are ● How they are misused by the unprincipled ● How they may be ethically applied

If people will be wicked, they had better of the two be so
from common vicious patterns…than from this deep and calm
source of delusion, which undermines the whole principle of
good; darkens the light, the candle of the Lord within, which
is to direct our step, and corrupts conscience which is the
guide of life.

(Bishop Butler)

Power: the possibility of imposing one's will upon the
behaviour of others.

(Max Weber)

THE OLDEST STORY EVER TOLD

Evolution has made us what we are and what we all too often are is – mugs. Unprincipled salespeople of every kind can use the well known tricks of the trade to make us respond to their wiles. Recognition of the tricks for what they are to some degree protects us against the potential harm to which our evolutionary history inadvertently has made us subject. In his brilliant and engaging book *Influence*, Robert Cialdini explains a wide range of recent historical con tricks which logic insists should not have happened.

Since the wiles of those whom Cialdini calls the 'compliance professionals' (unprincipled used car salespeople, estate agents and crooked politicians) are important and since we can build our defences against them, I intend to summarise some of their less salubrious tricks, drawing on the unpleasant phenomenon of religious cults for my examples.

THE WAGES OF SIN IS...

It was a hot day when the Branch Davidians died. Tragically few lived long enough that day to know how hot it was to become. Legal officers at last attempted to storm the compound from which the shots had come which had killed their colleagues and friends four months earlier. They began the attack at 0600; by noon Koresh's close associates were claimed to have been starting the fires which caused the deaths of the men, women and children who had believed that through giving their lives to Koresh they were giving them to God.

The victims were not religious nuts, nor were they unusually stupid. Many were extremely intelligent. Some were even trained in psychology. But wise or not, they fell victim to the deceit of one of the great evil manipulators of our age. The techniques which Koresh used were not special. They were precisely those techniques which we are hardwired to be ready to fall for. Ironically it was evolutionary advantage which gave him his victims.

THE EVOLUTION OF THE PATSY

Evolution occurs because a randomly acquired quality is useful. By 'useful' I mean that it helps the individual who has it to survive and to breed within the environmental conditions of the time and place. Through breeding the useful quality is passed down and spreads through the population. In time the majority of organisms show the trait in question. How is it that useful genetic endowments can become so damaging?

Suppose you lived in an area where malaria was endemic. Malaria weakens the individual and threatens life because an organism parasitises the red blood cells. If you happened to have blood cells which had developed a capacity to defend themselves from invasion, you might have an advantage which would enable you to outlive and outperform your neighbours. You would almost certainly leave more descendants and you would have passed on a legacy. You would have bequeathed to your offspring and to theirs a condition now known as sickle cell anaemia. While defence against the danger of malaria was the priority your descendants would thrive, but once the danger had passed the erstwhile life saver would have become the author of an agonising and crippling disease.

Similarly, there was a survival advantage in making speedy but sound decisions. Our ancestors who inherited the capacity to develop short cuts in analysing incoming information by recognising and responding to partial but critical cues were faster off the mark than their competitors and prospered in a dangerous world. Of course mistakes would be made, occasion-ally lethal ones, but little can be more deadly than pondering every situational variable as the sabretooth tiger is poised to spring. In general quick responses were, in evolutionary terms, good responses and our ancestors passed to us the tendency to what Cialdini calls the 'click-whirr' response.

Lucky us. Well sometimes.

Thanks to evolution we are capable of taking action without undue time for thought. Thanks to the same characteristic we often respond with little or no thought at all. We perceive the appropriate cue and click-whirr slides into action as readily as a kneejerk. That's not too much of a problem when, for example, after years developing a reputation for quality and innovation manufacturers and suppliers get us to buy on the strength of their name alone. Today, after a consistent history of excellence, Sony, BMW, Microsoft and others may have earned our unthink-ing allegiance to their names alone, but it doesn't end there.

We seek different satisfactions and divergent feelings about brand images always make some of us unmanageable. So a few of us slip under the wire. But there are tricks of any trade to which very few, if any, of us are immune and often we fail to recognise them when they're used. Then we are victims rather than buyers. Let me explain.

RECIPROCITY

Cialdini calls reciprocity, as it is exploited by the compliance professional, that old give and take…and take…and take. One of the redeeming features of the way that evolution has shaped our behaviour is that in social situations few of us are mean. Generosity can, however, be the undoing of those whose only intention is an innocent return, with interest, of a favour.

It is no coincidence that a synonym for 'thank you' in English is 'I am obliged to you' and those who have our worst interests at heart understand that better than most. 'I'm much obliged' is an archaic form of speech which is seldom heard outside the formal confines of the courtroom today, but what we no longer say we continue to live.

Few readers will not have experienced a situation in which reciprocity is expensive – even if it is a welcome expense. For example, you may walk into a bar with the intention of having just one quiet drink. An acquaintance sees you at the door and when you reach the bar you find that a glass of your regular poison is waiting for you. Can you still have that one drink and leave? Or do you reciprocate by buying a round which includes not only the buyer of your drink, but any friends and relations he or she happens to be with?

It wouldn't be a problem if we simply returned like for like. But most of us go further. Your neighbour invites you for a simple snack, you in your turn invite them for dinner. They ask you to a formal dinner party and the merrygoround of reciprocity goes into ever-growing cycles of two way traffic which threaten to bankrupt you both. 'No human society fails to support the rule – return the good turn with interest,' as Alvin Gouldner has written. Society is built on reciprocity. If you scratch my back, I am expected not merely to scratch yours, but to massage your shoulder and wipe your fevered brow into the bargain. At the level I have described such a response is warm, pleasant and relatively harmless; but in the hands of a villain, harmless it is not.

David Koresh was an apparently unpreposessing individual. He was, by numerous accounts, a scruffy religious maniac with a tendency to masturbation and a grubby schoolboy's predilection for talking about it, but he played on human preprogramming as a master. Among the Davidians indulgence in such delicacies as MacDonald's burgers or root beer was a sin. Koresh had an interesting view of sin, however – to him a sin was not so much what was done as who did it. He therefore retained for himself not only the right to commit any and all sins, in public and in private, but also the authority to permit others to indulge in the more minor peccadilloes.

Thus he would organise outings to the local burger bar and, having done a good turn of pandering to status and gluttony together, he would ask for little favours in return. Small things like the company of a prepubescent daughter in his bed. Clearly it takes more than a burger and a root beer under normal circumstances to enable a paedophile to buy a child, but the circumstances were far from normal. What was powerful already took on incredible force when the favour was a rare event which contrasted so strongly with normal haranguing and even physical abuse.

Reciprocity is so powerful that it overcomes the basic rule of behaviour – we like to do good only for those that we like. If we feel obligated we begin to like, if only for a short span those whom, under normal circumstances, we might reasonably detest. That is one of the many complex reasons why battered wives for so long cling to and even revere their vicious partners.

Of course, Koresh also offered his followers a route to never-ending felicity. What would be an acceptable tit for tat for the promise of paradise?

IT'S NICE TO BE NICE

It is an axiom of sales that people like to buy from those they like. Salespeople of the old school take this belief so much to heart that they seek to be everybody's friend by being jocular and congenial in all circumstances. The view of the 'commercial traveller' from Chaucer to Arthur Miller has been a source of jokes and affability for all occasions. Psychology suggests, however, that the situation is a little more complex.

There can be no doubt about the truth of the axiom – the

question is whether wisecraking and unlimited agreeable behaviour form the best way of building feelings of friendship. Those who describe themselves as 'morning people' like to rise early and they do so bursting with energy. They start the day with a smile on their face and a song or joke on their lips. They drive to distraction those of us who awaken slowly and are easily irritated until we painfully reach a mild condition of good humour once the streets are fully aired. The old style salesman, and it usually was a man, tended to have the same effect on me as did those who seemed to see it as their duty to try to 'cheer me up' a mere nanosecond after the crack of dawn.

Social psychology has shown that the easiest way to create a sense of rapport is share the mood, and since mood is intimately bound up with posture, even the posture of the other. Empathy is more amicable in the long run than sympathy.

The people we like most are those who are most like us. Study of wildlife shows that it is common, particularly as a prelude to mating, for animals to mirror each other's behaviour in an often complex ritual. Such behaviour mirrors the similarities which exist in a breeding species and build the bonds of the relationship. Social psychology and subsequently neurolinguistic programming (NLP) provide tools to build human relationships quickly through basically similar techniques.

Body language and NLP are discussed in Chapter 5. For the moment I would like to concentrate on abuse, which brings me unerringly back to Koresh.

Elias Porter showed many years ago that a common cause of marital problems was based on our assumption that those we love think as we do. When, rather than if, we discover that loved ones do not share either our most sacred beliefs or our most esteemed tastes, the trouble is likely to start. The diversity which makes evolution possible can cause as much dissention in the kitchen as it creates pleasure in the bedroom.

Koresh, as all cult leaders do, used the power of shared beliefs to bring his followers closer to each other. He selected his recruits from those who shared a deep and sincere belief in God. Further, he and his henchmen persuaded them to believe that they were to be among the 144,000 blessed of the Book of Revelation, who, through their belief and sacrifice, would be

God's chosen ones. Having gone thus far it was a short step to a belief in Koresh himself, not as a prophet or preacher, but as the son of God. This blasphemy retained its power in spite of Koresh's sexual behaviour and his nomination of himself as the 'masturbating messiah', partly because his followers had by this time burned too many boats to turn back and partly because Koresh developed in them a sense of dependence by persuading them that the world beyond the wires of Waco existed only to destroy the Davidians. Their only friends were within the compound and for such friends nothing was too great a sacrifice.

CONFORMITY, CONSISTENCY AND COMMITMENT

There is an old psychological experiment in which a group of people are ostensibly required to judge which is the longer of two lines of unequal size. I say 'ostensibly', because only one of the group is genuinely the subject of the experiment. The others are the stooges of the psychologists. A number of trials take place in which in spite of subtleties of difference easy unanimity of judgement is established.

Then two lines of obviously different lengths are shown. To the genuine subject's surprise the first to make the judgement gets it clearly wrong. Surprise turns to astonishment as one after the other each member of the group apparently makes the same mistake. Finally the subject is to make their choice. Most deny their own judgement and go along with the group decision regardless of how obviously wrong it is. They would rather be friendly than right. What is more, they rationalise their decision on the basis of 'different viewing angles' causing an illusion.

The drive toward conformity shows itself in all areas of human behaviour, from the similarity of clothing of teenagers seeking, ironically, to be different, to the shared belief of the institutionalised old that they are helpless.

Koresh expected his followers to accept conditions of hardship. An ascetic lifestyle was exacerbated by beatings and haranguing which lasted for many hours past exhaustion. As those who design 'hell weeks' at American universities are only too well aware, a hardship shared is a bond forged. And a bond once forged creates conformity even in the face of reason. For as long as Koresh could be sure that the 'opinion leaders' in his flock would obey his commandments, the rest were putty in his hands.

A parallel situation has existed in the British National Health Service for many years. Junior doctors traditionally work long hours, often to the point of exhaustion and beyond. Such work practices can only put at risk the well-being and even the lives of patients. The government, ever mindful of cost, decreed that junior doctors' hours of work should be gradually, far too gradually, reduced to 79 hours a week. (As an aside, would you choose to be flown in a plane piloted by an officer who was coming to the end of a 79-hour working week?) Even with a reluctant government finally converted toward marginal improvement there was opposition to reducing the hours – from senior doctors.

Senior doctors had, in their day, worked the exhausting routine of the junior doctor. They valued it. It was regarded, stupidly but unsurprisingly, as making them what they were today'. It was to be defended at all costs. Little matter if it had cost and continues to cost the lives of both patients and young, caring doctors.

So much is this myth part of medicine that a non-existent disease, adult death syndrome, has been created to explain the deaths of those doctors who are killed by the combination of overwork and guilt. Like hyperpyrexia UO (a high temperature of unknown origin) and heart failure, it serves the purpose of cloaking ignorance and stupidity with something which sounds, to the layperson at least, scientific and therefore respectable.

It is almost a law of anthropology that the severity of an initiation ceremony heightens the newcomers' commitment to the group. Psychologists know that this sense of belonging is carried forward to include a desire to see others experience no less as the price of entry. Through the high price demanded and paid, conformity is assured.

It is important to understand that although a high price may be demanded, a high reward is counter-productive. If you want me to own and thus repeat my actions I must believe that I did whatever I did because I chose to and not for a reward. Those who believe that you can buy acquiescence are right, but the cost of buying intrinsically unattractive behaviour rises with every repetition. However, if you can get others to take one small step in the direction which you desire by offering either no or minimal reward, they will take further and much bigger steps when you ask it of them. Let's look at how this works.

Cialdini explains a simple and much hidden fact of recent American history. Although those Americans who were captured in the Korean War withstood torture and ill-treatment with great courage, many, possibly all, of those who were captured by the less brutal Chinese were persuaded to commit small acts of disloyalty. The Chinese method was subtle and psychologically sound.

Rather than mistreat their prisoners physically, the Chinese put their faith in 'reeducation'. We tend to think of brainwashing as the source of much uncharacteristic behaviour. Endless interrogations, frequent beatings, incessant noise and constant artificial light are the tools of the brainwasher and American troops were well prepared to withstand these. The Chinese simply engaged their prisoners in polite political discussion. They were encouraged to express themselves freely. Their captors listened politely while they extolled the American way or attacked Maoism. There was disagreement, but it was civilised.

At the end of an early session the Chinese would gravely thank the prisoners for their interesting input. Then the first stage of the trap was sprung.

'You make America sound like a paradise. Has your system no shortcomings?'

An apparently reasonable question from a reasonable person. If the answer indicated that America was indeed a paradise on earth a couple of more specific questions might be inserted.

'Is there no poverty at all? No unemployment?'

The questions were never allowed to sound like a challenge, they simply indicated the puzzlement of a seeker after truth. The prisoner would often admit that there was some poverty and that there was indeed unemployment. There was no strong reaction to this information, but the Chinese official would ask for a small favour. For the next discussion would the American, in the interests of completeness, jot down a few shortcomings of the capitalist system. If the prisoner did as requested he was hooked.

When we are persuaded to take action against our inclination we have to justify that action to ourselves. Collaboration with an enemy, even minor collaboration, requires considerable justification.

The easiest way to reduce the dissonance between our role as soldier and our cooperation is to regard the behaviour as coming from our highest motives. We are right and they are wrong, but part of our rightness lies in our ability to be honest even when the truth is unpalatable. Once we have developed a self-image of honesty we can readily be persuaded to take any step consistent with that self-image. The prisoner is subsequently asked to write a short essay on the shortcomings of the American way of life – he complies. Asked to list the, admittedly few, superior characteristics of Marxism – he does so. Asked to broadcast an anti-war message and he does that too. We are all pacifists when we are the immediate victims of war. Thus honesty and decency slip imperceptibly into treason.

Koresh used this with his followers even to the extent of having them provide his bedmates from among their youngest daughters. He started by asking them to offer themselves to God's service. A vague request, but one which implied a very strong and specific self-image. In the service of God he asked people to cut themselves free from those heathenish friends and relatives who tempted them away from the highway of the Lord. That done, he demanded that they leave home and country and join his community. Once there and subject to all the other carefully designed psychological pressures, virtually no demand could be refused. Give their money to the common wealth? – they gave freely. Obey the every word of the new messiah? – they obeyed and praised the Lord. Hand over your daughter to breed sons of the son of God? – sadly they complied and believed it virtue. Die to demonstrate your total commitment? – tragically they did so.

We accept inner responsibility for our actions and we continue to behave consistently with them when we do what we do in the absence of strong external pressure, reward or sanction.

Jonathon Freedman carried out an experiment which shows that we don't need to be very old for this effect to be powerful. He invited young children to play with a range of toys. There was one restriction. Half of the children were told: 'Don't play with the robot or you will be severely punished.' The remainder were told: 'Don't play with the robot because it's wrong to do so.'

Both groups of children obeyed and the robot stood untouched. Later, however, the children were given another opportunity to play. Those who had been threatened with punishment played with the robot as soon as experimenters' backs were turned and, apparently at least, the chance was given. Those who had been told that, for some unexplained reason, playing with the robot was wrong continued to leave it severely alone. This little experiment has a moral which all parents might like to think about.

A lot of our dependence on authority, and much of our acquies-cence to dictators, is blamed by the chattering classes on Aristotle and/or the Roman Catholic Church. If it were that easy it wouldn't be a problem.

AUTHORITY, AUTHORITY, WHO'S GOT THE AUTHORITY?

Once again evolution has hardwired us and the institutions merely take advantage of our nature. They mould us within limits, they don't create us.

During what an American friend of mine calls 'the late, great unpleasantness', the Nazis were guilty of atrocities which many of us believe placed them way apart from humanity. What on earth, or beyond it, could drive anyone to such foul actions? Can you accept the frequently offered defence: 'I was only obeying orders'?

Common sense and common decency combine to say 'no'. What does psychological research say?

Come and help me with an experiment. Join, if you will a number of other volunteers and wait for the experiment to begin.

In the room where you sit, waiting for the experiment to begin, is a group of white-coated psychologists. They seem to be waiting for the arrival of someone more important. They talk to each other in hushed tones. Occasionally the importance of the group is accented by your hearing one addressed as 'doctor' or even 'professor'. And yet...

They keep glancing nervously toward the door of the room as they talk together quietly, yet somehow a little nervously. They are apologetic about the delay, but they imply that to start without 'the governor' would be impossible. As time passes their anxiety grows, but it is clear that to start would take more courage than they have between them. Whoever is finally to enter through that door must be someone of unique importance.

At last the door opens and a distinguished looking man in a dark suit enters. He is pleasant to you and the other volunteers, but is dismissive and patronising to the assembled psychologists. He gives orders which are obeyed with dispatch. Obviously he is a man used to being obeyed.

You are told that the experiment is to test the effectiveness of 'punishment as a means to promoting learning'. You are probably relieved to hear that you are to administer rather than receive the punishment.

Through a one-way mirror you can see the subject of the experiment. He is a man of late middle age seated at a desk. Before him is a microphone.

The equipment which you will use in the experiment is simple. A handle is turned and a needle moves around a gauge. The gauge is marked in turn 'Very Mild Shock', 'Mild Shock', 'Moderate Shock', 'Shock', 'Severe Shock', and the last position is marked simply 'Danger'.

Your role is explained as that of 'teacher'. The subject will be tested on information which he has been set to learn. For any incorrect answer you will be required to administer an electric shock by turning the handle. The subject cannot see you during the experiment, but thanks to the one-way glass and the microphone you are able both to see and hear all that happens.

The experiment begins. Occasionally a wrong answer is given. The experimenter instructs you to administer a shock. You see and hear the subject's response to pain. As time passes and errors become more frequent you are told to administer increasingly stronger voltages.

Time passes, neither comfortably for you nor for your victim.

The subject's early and mild reactions are now being replaced by cries of real pain. As you obey the instruction to increase the level of shock the pain is evident in the subject's shouts. He screams, babbles almost incoherently about his severe heart condition, begs for the experiment to stop, even sobs that if it continues he will not live to see his grandchildren again.

If you indicate any wish to stop the experiment you are quietly but firmly told: 'The experiment must continue. Administer the shock.'

Would you stop? Or would you continue until you saw and heard for yourself that what you had been doing 'under orders' had led to serious injury or even death?

I am sure that you and I would both be absolutely certain that we would not have allowed such an inhuman activity to continue. We would have firmly put an end to the experiment at an early stage, or even refused to take part at all once we were aware of what was expected of us.

You and I may be right, but we have the confidence in our behaviour which comes from not having been tested. But if we are right we are in the minority. When the experiment has been carried out, approximately seven out of ten have responded to perceived authority by continuing to the bitter end. And the end in this case is the collapse, or even the 'death' of the victim.

Of course, the experiment is a fake. The victim is an actor. The apparatus is a box, a wheel, a dial and nothing more. No shocks are administered other than the shock of finding that a majority of sane, reasonable people, drawn from all stratas of society, will respond to perceived authority and careful use of language to the extent of torturing and even killing a fellow being.

Such is the power of authority.

The lesson for us should be plain. The appropriate mindset for those who wish to influence behaviour is one of assertiveness and authority. Too often the salesperson, the manager, the lover or the parent seeks to influence behaviour by being a supplicant. There is strong evidence that the appropriate relationship between 'salesperson' and 'buyer' is one in which the 'buyer' is just a little in awe of the other. A mild dominance, self-confidence and personal prestige are appropriate to the character of the 'salesperson' in every walk of business and social life. Not arrogance, not obnoxiousness, but confidence.

I will argue that the appropriate level of assertiveness will come most readily from understanding the psychological processes which are taking place, and applying certain skills with confidence, proficiency and sensitivity.

The manager or leader is given status both by the hierarchy in which they operate and by relatively greater experience or knowledge. The relative status of salesperson and customer needs to be that of equals in status who are cooperating in exploring the possibility of the product, service or idea being applied to the benefit of both. Or the customer or client should feel just a little in awe of the salesperson, at least in the salesperson's field of expertise. This feeling of awe can be developed by two strategies. Both are in my view essential.

First, the marketing strategy must be designed to raise the status and reputation of the organisation, its products and services and above all of its people. The brash, the pushy, the insensitive and the downright stupid must automatically create in the client mind Hoover's famous riposte:

> Slick salesman: 'I represent the XYZ Corporation.'
> Hoover: 'No sir. I know your company. You misrepresent the XYZ Corporation.'

Secondly, the salesperson or influencer must develop for themselves the status and reputation of a consultant with total knowledge of the client needs, their own product or service and competitive strengths and weaknesses. They must engender trust by becoming one to whom the client/customer turns for reliable information. This image of being a specialist must not then be destroyed by the use of cheap and nasty sales techniques which are obvious to all but the most naive. Methods used must be supportive of the image portrayed, and that means they are flexible, sensitive, gentle and research based.

The truly professional salesperson uses aikido where the old-style slugger would try for his 'honey punch' which, if it failed, would put him right out of the contest. And persuasion remains and always will remain a contest. No idea, product or service is the total ideal, the *non pareil*. Always there is competition. There are others who seek to show how their products or ideas meet more closely the buyer's needs. More importantly, there is competition within the buyer themselves.

Resistance to change, valued past experience, apathy or ignorance, any or all may be present. This book will teach you, step by step how to deal with all of the above and more as you build a superior relationship with those you seek to influence.

THERE'S NOT A LOT OF IT ABOUT

Koresh relied heavily, as do many religious fundamentalists, on the Book of Revelation and the Apocrypha for the fuel of his sermons. Both are esoteric and fuel the insanity of the wild-eyed fanatic. But they served another purpose for Koresh.

The human organism, like all mammals, is preprogrammed to compete vigorously for scarce resources. Altruism is not unknown in nature, but like big fierce animals it is rare. Although the Book of Revelation and the Apocrypha are in different testaments, they are both elitist. One declares and the other hints that tickets for entry into heaven are in short supply. Koresh and his ilk promise their followers the certainty of a place among the chosen and use scarcity as a tool of compliance. As a vicious psychopath, Koresh had another form of scarce resource which he doled out illiberally. Occasionally, and far from frequently, he was nice to people.

The used car salesperson knows the value of scarcity. Fail to buy that pristine Triumph Stag and you may be sure that one exactly like it will never appear on the market again. A now highly respected professor of psychology worked his way through college by spending much of his free time selling cars. He was doing pretty well, but thought that as a student of human behaviour he ought to be able to do much better.

Most dealerships put out a weekly advertisement which is little more than a stocklist. Customer's, most of whom have a clear idea of the make, model and year that they want to buy, peruse the lists, and since a wasted journey is to be avoided if possible, they telephone to check that their heart's desire is still in stock. When he received such calls our psychology student began to use what he'd learned. First he would make an appointment for the prospect to view the car, but – and here is the use of scarcity – all potential customers who had expressed an interest in a particular vehicle were invited to attend at the same time. Having created a small scrum around the car in question, our psychologist/salesman would, with due formality, check who had been the first to arrive and would attend to them.

With the car in such demand, it was easy to push the first prospect into a buying decision. What's more, there was no haggling over price. After all, it was probable that while he argued someone else would offer the asking price or better. The sale and maximum commission were assured, but that's not all.

There is a theory in psychology called 'cognitive dissonance'. Cognitive dissonance says, among other things, that the grass is only greener on the other side until it is clear that you are stuck with what you have. I might dream of owning a Rolls-Royce, but since my battered Renault is all I can afford I tend to think more highly of it than I would if the world were my oyster. For every buyer pushed into a hasty deal by scarcity, there is a

disappointed would-be purchaser. It was when dealing with the
disappointed that our psychology student moved from the
merely underhand to something approaching compliance
genius.

Young and quick on his feet, he speedily turned his attention
from the triumphant buyer to the disappointed buyers-in-
waiting. He would assure them that he was delighted that they
had not made the mistake of buying the desired car. Beautiful
example of its marque that it was, he had something better to
show them. Having been denied a scarce resource, they looked,
tested and tried whatever was now on offer. Their desire to steal
a march on the one who had so recently 'stolen' their heart's
desire from under their noses was so strong that they readily
identified and enhanced the advantages of the alternative. Thus
two sales – at least – were made for the effort of one.

Scarcity is a powerful tool of influence. Scarcity used
creatively and combined with cognitive dissonance has millions
of years of human evolution straining to give, thinking it is getting, two for the price of one.

**FRIENDSHIP AND
SOCIAL
VALIDATION**

Another inheritance which is a mixed blessing is our need for
social validation of our behaviour. Charities in particular like to
list their better known supporters in order that, in an attempt to
align ourselves, however fragilely, with the most respected in
society, we will dig deeeply into our pockets. When less well
known collectors are used they are required to collect close to,
but excluding, their own homes. In this way social validation and
friendship are combined. But members of cults do not enjoy
social support for their actions, so what do the Koreshes of this
world do to exploit this human need?

For centuries there has been a tendency for religious groups
who held extreme views to move away from the mainstream and
into the wilderness. Separated from society in general,
surrounded only by those who hold similar views, it is easy for
the most extreme beliefs to grow and flourish. Thus Jim Jones
led his followers into the jungles of Guyana before he organised
their slaughter when society, in the form of the press and a
Congressional investigation, followed them all the way to their
Central American retreat.

Similarly, Koresh established a series of encampments, moving away from each in turn as society intervened, until the last, tragic resting place at Waco. Within the wire the only social approbation available was from fellow believers and the fellow believers whose views counted were those who held the most extreme pro-Koresh beliefs, including his right to indulge in paedophilia.

Those who demurred were ostracised, savagely beaten and finally (and fortunately) cast out into what they had been brainwashed to believe was a hostile world. Significantly, those who most easily broke with Koresh were trusted lieutenants who had been delegated responsibility for the continuance of an early settlement in far off Australia.

Interestingly, the need for social validation is one which varies from individual to individual to a degree far greater than any 'click-whirr' response. Some of us need to feel that we have other people's approval for everything we do. Others are happy to let the world and its opinions go hang.

It is important to understand that individual susceptibility to the insidious 'click-whirr' of evolutionary hardwiring has nothing to do with intelligence or emotional stability. We are all, to a greater or lesser degree, patsies. To be aware of the danger gives some protection, but not always enough.

SUMMARY

Genetic evolution has hard wired us to be patsies.

Politicians, religious leaders and unscrupulous sales people use this knowledge improperly. That does not mean that it cannot be applied ethically. Technology is neutral. Knowledge, properly applied, is virtue. At the very least we ought to understand the tools which the ungodly are using with total disregard for ethics or morality. That way we may be able to protect ourselves and those we care for from some of the compliance professionals' insidious wiles.

I have concentrated in this chapter on how these otherwise valid tools of influence are misused, leading to the abuse of those who become their victims. Let me finish with a simple rule for their ethical use.

Any influence tool is ethical as long as one thing is borne carefully and consistently in mind. If you can create a genuine win/win situation by ensuring that the outcome you seek meets the needs or desires of the other person in a way which will give them something important which they want, then you need not question the means. And that leads us neatly into the next chapter.

Ethical Sales Skills for Everyone   3

WHAT YOU WILL GAIN FROM THIS CHAPTER

● How to listen
● How to ask questions
● How to structure sales presentations to meet the needs of the listener
● How to handle emotional outbursts
● How to deal with obstacles and objections without appearing to be a smart alec
● How to close the sale without pressure

It is what you do **and** *the way that you do it.*

The impact of the information economy will be most strongly felt in the area of sales. Customers, whether business buyers, users or consumers, are looking for a new kind of relationship with their suppliers. They are starting to miss the old educational role of the salesperson which has been for so long ignored by the pile 'em high, sell 'em cheap culture into which we have talked ourselves.

Gradually and perhaps too slowly, people are beginning to

appreciate that the cost of doing business has to do with more than just the price of goods or the discounts offered. Those who truly seek quality are coming to understand that their ability to provide it is a function of the relationship which they have with their suppliers. GIGO, garbage in – garbage out, is coming to be recognised as an inexorable law of far wider application than the input of data into a computer.

There is a chain between supplier and consumer in which every step is an opportunity to add value in terms of quality of product and service. To add value every step of the way requires that the seller, whether they sell products, services or ideas, must target all they say and do to delivering value in terms of meeting or exceding the known and predicted needs of the organisation or individual. That means that those who intend to influence the behaviour of others are dependent on planning.

An old colleague of mine used to say that forecasting may be defined as what would have happened if what did happen didn't. Something similar may be said of planning which is based on insufficient or dubious knowledge.

If the pile 'em high, sell 'em cheap brigade base their approach on the idea that there will always be a market for rubbish, they are right. There will always be those who can afford nothing but rubbish. But if they believe that the market for rubbish is huge and will continue to expand, they are wrong. As technology and marketing combine to ensure ever higher quality, expectations increase everywhere.

For example, cars in general have improved in the key areas of reliability, performance and safety to a degree undreamed of only 10 years ago. Of course we still get the dreaded 'Friday car' now and again, but whether you buy top of the range, middle or what used to be the old jokes of the car imports, today you can buy with confidence. If you doubt me, look and see what good things the Consumers' Association has to say these days about Skoda quality.

Exceeding the buyer's desires is hardly more than acceptable in the new business world. The essential is, however, to do so economically – any buffoon can get business or compliance by giving the world away and then lying down and asking the world to walk all over them.

To meet, or better yet exceed another's wants is dependent on knowledge. Wants are volatile and what delights me today will offer me no great pleasure tomorrow – or perhaps it will delight me until the end of my days. If you want to delight me today *and* tomorrow you need to know which of my sources of delight are unchanging and which are new. If we have a relationship characterised by high levels of mutual trust and openness, I will give you all the information that you need to bind me to you or your firm for life. That relationship is a direct function of how well you add personal value by consistently understanding and meeting my needs.

In short, the current and future role of the salesperson must be one of building long-term relationships in the initial sales process, so that repeat and referral sales are assured and the salesperson's time may be applied to enhancing the quality of the service, product and relationship.

The sales manager has a unique advantage in the postindustrial society. Among managers in the smokestack economies of the past only the sales manager was expected to manage a specialist team at something more than arm's length. The skills which enabled the successful sales manager to support and enthuse a dispersed team are worth considering in the search for techniques and capabilities which will facilitate the future management of telecommuters and knowledge workers.

Similarly, the skills of the best sales managers have always been directed at the development and accelerated move toward autonomy of the entire salesforce, and development skills have been applied on the basis of carefully defined individual need. This coaching skill will be an essential prerequisite to the growth of effective empowerment.

Many companies of the future will survive and prosper by making fuller and more imaginative use of all their resources, human and otherwise. As Drucker and others have pointed out, the day of the intrapreneur is at hand. The skills implicit in the highest standards of sales and sales management will enable the creative specialist to sell his good ideas at every level within and outside the organisation.

Leadership skills will need to evolve to take account of the different needs of an information society. With quality and excellence increasingly recognised and demanded as the ultimate determinants of competitive advantage and the need to compete globally even on your own doorstep, the same is true of selling techniques. Indeed, 20 years ago General Motors Overseas Corporation recognised the tie-in between leadership and sales skills by mandating sales training for all senior executives.

Everybody is a salesperson sometimes. You sell when you build enthusiasm for your exciting new idea. You sell when you persuade someone to take on an undesirable, but essential duty. You sell when you convince the boss that you are worth a substantial raise – and you sell when you convince me that I am not worth a raise this time without damaging my motivation to perform in the future.

Salespeople will need to focus beyond the immediate sale and concentrate, as I have suggested above, on the building of relationships. This doesn't mean that the immediate sale is unimportant. Quite the contrary, you have to make the sale. It is the only way you can prove to the buyer that you can deliver. Everything other than performance is merely a parcel of promises. Make it a resolution now. You can and will win them all as long as your product, idea or service can truly deliver the goods and the return makes the effort worthwhile.

LISTENING SKILLS

Too often listening skills are taught in a way that reminds me of Auntie Edna. All my life I have claimed to love what I called 'good music'. I included under the heading 'good music' some jazz and the great performers of what are called the 'standards', especially Sinatra and Ella Fitzgerald, but my great love was always the classics: Bach, Mozart, Beethoven. If Auntie Edna came into a room where I was playing records she would immediately sit down and put on her listening face. Her expression took on an intensity and her posture was tense. She would gaze into the far distance, apparently in rapt attention. Very impressive to look at, but it didn't mean a thing. Her preferred listening was the Jimmy Young programme.

In most training programmes participants are told to *listen*. They put on Auntie Edna faces and do their honest best to go against their nature. Sadly, the mind doesn't work in a way which makes concentrated, inactive listening possible.

Listening is an active process. What is more, it is sometimes focused and sometimes diffuse. Research has shown that what enables us to remember information is not concentration, but processing. We need to practise in/out listening, taking in information and relaxing as your mind plays with it. Above all, we need to process the information and link ideas in a way which makes them memorable and spurs new, exciting inspirations.

Listening requires not concentrated silence, but intelligent interjections. Those interjections typically are of two types:

● Supportive actions to encourage the expression of further thoughts and feelings such as smiles, nods or verbal encouragement – of the 'that's interesting, please tell me more' variety.
● Sensible and relevant questions.

Salespeople have always been taught, rightly, that they should be in control of the discussion. They have also been advised that the best way to take and keep control is by asking questions – equally true. In relationship selling the vital thing is not to turn a discussion into an interrogation. Questions should be used sensitively to enable the other to talk freely about what they feel, think and want. That means that the flow through open questions (how did that make you feel?) and closed questions (how many people were involved?) and yes/no questions (are you unhappy with the present situation?) to occasional leading questions (if I can show you how to invest with absolute security and instant access would that meet your needs?) has to be supported with progress test questions.

VE ARE ASKING ZE QUESTIONS!

Progress test questions are an essential tool in moving the 'buyer' step by step, comfortably and seamlessly toward agreement – but they must be used sensitively. The essential difference between what is generally taught and what is offered in this book is that the individual or group that you are seeking to influence go through a distinct and well studied, step-by-step thinking process. If we do nothing to impede their movement, and a little to ease it, they will reach the final point, that of agreeing to what you want, comfortably and without any sense of pressure. Occasionally, to be sure that the process has been comfortably facilitated, you need to ask for confirmation. That's why progress test questions were born.

Let me explain with the beginning of the process.

Structure speaks loudest of all

The next chapter will explain cognitive mapping and the practical and academic research which supports it. For the moment I think it will be most helpful if I concentrate on the 'how to', including the use of progress test questions.

If somebody, anybody, wants me to do something different I can be pardoned if my first reaction is to wonder: 'What's in it for me?' If, however, I was convinced that you, in trying to change my behaviour, were showing me how the change would bring me what I want, that very sensible question would be answered in the positive – at least provisionally – until I had evaluated your idea in detail. If I want to do this, I need to hear it in detail, so you have my favourable attention.

How, then, are you to convince me that you have my interests and *only* my interests at heart? Simple. I am assuming that now we have had the preliminary discussion. You have a clear idea of my wants, and you have satisfied yourself that your product, service or idea can play a significant part in helping to satisfy them. (If you can't help me to achieve something that I want, forget it. I can help you to become a better con artist, but I don't choose to. My reason for this apparent high moral tone is pragmatic not ethical. Con me this time and you forfeit the ability to convince me in the future.)

So can you help me to my heart's desire? Since this is now the central core of everything that follows, make sure that I really want what you offer. At this stage the progress test question is mandatory. Success depends on a positive answer.

'From what you've told me it is essential to you to find a way of getting more business which is professional, ethical and congruent with your role. (Buyer's objective) Have I got it right?

(Progress test question) Because if so I think I can help you.'

If the answer is by some mischance 'no', then you return to listening to find out what it is that is really wanted that you can help to achieve.

'Really. I'm sorry I misunderstood. What are you looking for right now?'

But 999 times out of 1000 you will have got it right and having got it right you have, and can keep, the other's favourable attention. You can move on to the next stage.

Sometimes the buyer will be apathetic. Their key goal deep-down is inertia. What they would really like is that you should say: 'Do nowt and all that you desire will come to you as if by magic'. This attitude is not as unreasonable as it appears.

Whatever we do, we do for a very simple reason – it works for us. Sometimes I am painfully aware that what has worked in the past works no longer and I am actively seeking to change, but often I am bound emotionally and pragmatically to the past, and all I want is to return to the comfortable world of days gone by when my old behaviour played a part in giving me what success I have enjoyed in life.

In the latter situation you need to shake my apathy if you want me to consider a change. But changing apathy into action is an area of human interaction replete with emotional danger. If you want to keep my favourable attention you had better not upset me by denigrating the behaviours which brought me past success.

When I ask participants on my training programmes what they do in this situation, they correctly answer that they explain what has changed in the world which makes the old behaviour no longer desirable. But the devil is in the detail. The key to success lies in the choice of changing conditions.

Only conditions which are neutral should ever be used to shake apathy. They should be the agreed behaviour of other people or things. They should be neither in the control of you or your listener. Clearly they should not be in your control, because if you are doing something different which now causes pain to your buyer the solution is simple. Stop it right now!

If, on the other hand, the conditions are within the buyer's control, for example they have introduced a new system with

which their old behaviour is inconsistent, you are accusing them
of idiocy. To do six inconsistent things before breakfast may be
typical human behaviour, but we hate to be reminded of it. I see
myself as a rational being who thinks things through. Indicate
that you believe otherwise and you have a fight on your hands. If
you want to keep someone's favourable attention, tie in your
conditions to the behaviour of other people or things.

'Clients have some funny ideas. They don't expect
professional advisers to sell their services using recognisable
sales techniques. They expect us to talk like surgeons not
salespeople.' (Conditions, or what the buyer of your idea is up
against)

'This means that the sales techniques which are taught on
most training courses are totally inappropriate for getting
professional assignments. Yet these unprofessional, unnatural
techniques are all that we usually have access to and we can
lose a lot of business as a result.' (Losses to the listener
experienced not through their stupidity but because of the
expectations (perhaps unreasonable) of others.)

Now note that the listener has every reason to recognise the
need to do something different. More so if you add a progress
test question:

'Is that what sometimes happens to you?'

If you agree by now both on the desired outcome and on the
cause of the problem, the buyer should welcome any suggestion
you care to make which will help. But the devil, or maybe an
angel, is again in the detail. Did you notice something
interesting about the losses resulting from the conditions?

They were linked logically together. If the first is a true
consequence of the conditions the second, since it is a
consequence of the first, must always be true. And that second
loss leads logically to the exact opposite of what it is that the
listener wants. Now we've done it. We've got the listener to
agree that they want something and we've convinced them that
with things as they are they cannot have it. That should really
cheer them up! Let's raise their spirits a little.

'The problem can be avoided.'

In fact, let's give them a little more to hope for:

'You can sell to buyers successfully without them realising

that you are selling at all (Benefit) if you plan and deliver the presentation of your ideas entirely from the buyer's point of view.' (My good idea that I want you to 'buy')

Please note that I have introduced my good idea with a benefit. This is not to sell the idea. The single benefit is far too weak for that. What I am selling at this stage is nothing more than to get you to go on listening (or reading).

Many years ago I was a District Manager for General Motors. My job was specifically to get my 30 or so dealers to buy ever-increasing amounts of General Motors products without appearing to sell to them. (Company policy was that their field managers were to be perceived as 'gentlemen, not salesmen'. For that reason a senior manager had the occasional responsibility to take new recruits out for the day to ensure that we could get drunk like gentlemen.) To sell without selling I used what we called the 'pull-through effect'. I advised dealers on how to increase their business. With increased sales they needed more stock. With increased profits they wanted more stock, and I never had to ask for an order.

I did, however, need to ask for something, and in the early stages that caused me a few problems.

In my day the vast majority of car dealerships were family concerns. For decades they had regarded the 'books' as sacred objects to be kept safe from the prying eyes of outsiders. I had 30 dealers to cover which meant that my visits could either be brief or infrequent. I needed a short cut to giving good advice and the only short cut available was a detailed analysis of the books. If I asked to see them they were brought out of the safe and held closely to the dealer's chest, while he grudgingly asked: 'What do you want to know?'

As any accountant will tell you, although there are certain very important financial ratios, meaningful analysis of financial and management accounts is a little like chess. You need to be able to take in the whole board at a glance. I needed to see those books.

One day I chanced to ask in a slightly different way:

'I know that you're busy. So that I don't waste your time with irrelevant questions, may I look at your accounts?'

They were handed over without demur. Simple and obvious?

Yes, but not so simple and obvious that this dill-brain didn't take weeks of frustration and a chance way of expressing a simple request to learn an important lesson. If you want someone to do something for you, even if it's only to listen to you, tell them what's in it for them. The real sell, of course, comes later.

When you get to the 'how' – your idea, product or service – if you have laid the groundwork effectively the listener will want to hear all the details which are relevant to the attainment of their goal. (If you doubt this, consider the vast range of magazines 'What This' and 'Which That' existing solely to provide product information for buyers and dreamers.) Explain the relevant features. Show what support or service back-up you can give. Tell, if you have their permission, about the high status users and quote the positive things that they say about your offering. Demonstrate any features which give evidence that the buyer will be able to make the most of the situation if they say 'yes'. And they will say 'yes', because you link a benefit to the last feature and build on a logical structure of benefits which lead unerringly and inescapably to the achievement of the buyer's goal.

Once you have completed the structure, stop talking and wait for them to say 'yes please'. No fancy and overused closing techniques, just give space in which to mull over your offering and realise that it is the answer to their unspoken prayers.

Never be the first to speak when you have completed the presentation of your good idea. Wait patiently, letting the pressure on the other person imperceptibly grow. If instead of indicating compliance they raise an objection, welcome it as an indication of aroused interest. Psychologically an objection is an indicator of your failure to provide enough information, which is why Italians say *Chi disprezza compra* (who criticises buys). The speed with which they buy, of course, is a function of how well you handle their objections.

A TECHNIQUE CALLED SARAH

No matter how careful you are, regardless of the sensitivity which you show toward others' needs and feelings, there will be rare but unavoidable times when suddenly and for no obvious reason, the listener shows signs of disagreement and even anger. By word or gesture he will indicate that you have done or said something which triggers a negative response. It will seldom be clear to you where you went off track. You are choosing your words for the best possible effect, so you can hardly help but be taken by surprise if they cause an adverse reaction.

Salespeople, managers and speakers at conferences, seeing the signs, break simultaneously into a sweat and a gallop. They feel that if only they can finish what they are saying all will be well. After all, they have an unanswerable, logical case which they have thought through with great care. If only they get all our logic expressed for the customer's consideration, the misunderstanding, whatever it may be, will be resolved and the customer will be happy once more and the order assured.

Unfortunately, trying to deal with emotions with logic alone does not work. Think about those times when you get upset for little or no reason. If someone tries to change your mood with logic, do you listen to them? If you are anything like me you do not. What I do is to ignore what is being said or use it selectively to help me to think of all the convincing reasons why I am right to feel as I do. The more others try to make me feel better with their appeals to logic the worse I feel, and the worse I feel the more aggressive I become. It seems that they have no interest in what I feel or what I am thinking and that makes me mad. They can gabble on all they please, but I am not listening. I nurse my grievance and wait until they pause for breath and then I let them have it. Meanwhile nothing that they say enters my consciousness unless it adds fuel to my fire of indignation.

When things start to go off the rails and signs of roused emotions appear, think SARAH.

Do not talk faster, in fact do not talk at all. Give the listener the opportunity to express their feelings. You understand the psychological pressure of silence – let it work for you. No matter how painful the silence seems, there is absolutely nothing you can usefully say. If the silence is uncomfortable to you it is worse for the listener. After all, you are silent for a reason. You want to force them to say something, anything which will help you eventually to get back on track. Hold your tongue and within seconds (it will feel like minutes) your listener will break the silence. When they do…

Stop talking

Active listening

Listen as if your life depends on understanding how your customer feels and what they think. Make no attempts to second guess; always accept what is said as if it were true. Most of all, do not listen to customer objections with the intention of hearing some small error which enables you to think, 'Got you, you bastard!' followed by an attempt to devastate the listener with your lucidity and grasp of facts.

For this, usually brief, interjection you do not need to practise in/out listening. Instead, listen and watch for the expression of feelings. Feelings are facts in any situation; in this case it is your customer's feelings which are the most salient facts of all. So when they have stopped talking...

Reflect content or feeling

Paraphrase a key statement your customer has made to demonstrate that you really have been listening. Say it musingly to show that you are carefully considering what is being said and not doing parrot-like imitations. If nothing coherent enough has been said, then reflect what is clear to you about what the client is feeling:

'You are very upset.'
'You feel that it is unfair?'
'Something I've said has made you angry.'

If you reflect feeling, wait for a response. The listener will almost certainly now expand on what the problem is and, if you have remained concerned but calm, you will find that the client becomes a little calmer too, as they realise that there is no need to try to convince you of the validity of the arguments that they have been rehearsing internally to justify the mood swing. When they are ready...

Act with empathy

Show them that you accept that others have an absolute right to feel any way they please. They may in fact be wrong. They may have completely misunderstood. You may have inadvertently triggered a prejudice of which any right-minded person would be ashamed. Nonetheless, they have an absolute right as individuals to deal with their own problems their own way. But be sure you can tell the difference between empathy and sympathy and take care that you never express sympathy – 'You are absolutely right to feel as you do' – when you intend to convey empathy – 'You have an absolute right to feel as you do.' The devil is again in the detail and the difference allows you, after expressing empathy, to correct their thinking and consequently change their feeling. Once you have shown sympathy you are locked into their feeling. no matter how injurious it is to your case.

Empathy is shown in expressions like:

'I can understand you feeling that way, many people do'

or

'I can understand your concern, obviously I haven't made clear...'

When your calm, sensitive handling of the situation has made it easy for your client to listen to reason again, deal with any objections raised. Always deal with what your client says. Never try to second guess 'what they really mean'. You will almost certainly get it wrong. Even if you were to get it right, you will destroy the belief that you have been listening carefully and with empathy and understanding.

Handle objections

Research over the last 60 years has shown that objections can be classified and has identified the most appropriate tactics for handling each type. Avoid like the proverbial plague the suggestion that you should turn an objection into a so-called trial close. If a salesperson says to me, 'If I could satisfy you on that point would you buy today?' or some similar rigmarole learned parrot fashion, I feel that I am being tricked and placed under unfair pressure. My answer is likely to be along the lines of:

OBJECTIONS AND OBSTACLES

'I wouldn't buy from you while you are topologically a torus.'

Which, if you think about it, is an unbearably twee way of saying something which, outside of books, is refreshingly and satisfyingly vulgar.

The following are the objections which most frequently occur.

Something appears to cost too much when it seems to offer insufficient benefit for the price to be paid in money or effort. Use more benefits to demonstrate that your product or idea offers exceptional value.

Price

Any worthwhile idea will deliver many benefits which will not fit into the logical flow toward the achievement of your listener's key goals. You will not, therefore, be using them as the main argument for compliance. Use them when the price obstacle arises to convince your listener that you are providing exceptional added value.

'I can see your problem and really it's my fault. I should have explained that because this approach only varies in detail from what you do normally, it is easy for you to adapt it to your way of presenting ideas. This means that it feels and sounds perfectly natural, which helps the client to feel good too. This leads to increased business because the client who feels at ease with you seldom wants to risk talking to salespeople who use a pressure approach. Have I made it clearer now?'

Habit

'We've always done it this way, and it works' is not an invitation for you to focus on why the old way is stupid and your idea is infinitely better. It does give you the opportunity, however, to recognise that you have not shown sufficiently clearly how the changes in the environment in which your customer operates are such that major problems may result in the future if steps are not taken now. It may be that your initial assessment was that the listener would welcome the opportunity to change when, in reality, the behaviour was more ingrained than you thought. If you didn't use neutral conditions when you presented the idea the first time, now is your opportunity to make good the omission. When you do, be sure to take the blame for your failure. Never allow your listener to believe that you failed to explain something because you thought that anyone with half a brain would see that for themselves.

You will, of course, need to convince the listener that the product or service which you are advocating will be effective in today's changed or changing conditions.

'Yes, I can see why you feel that way. The old ways are always more comfortable. I suppose that I am really suggesting this new approach because it seems to me that clients are increasingly mistrustful of consultants and react badly to anything which they believe to be pressure selling. Have you found that they're getting more difficult to convince?'

Competition

'We have always been happy with our present supplier' is asking you to expand on what is unique about your offer. I am sure that you are aware that the key to a successful marketing plan is the identification of a USP (unique selling proposition). 'Me too' ideas only have an appeal if they are, at greatly reduced price.

Your listener is asking you to give more detail about the uniqueness of your product, idea or service. Concentrate on what it is that you offer that gives the competitive edge. Any feature of your service which is unique should be explained in detail from the user's point of view. Make it absolutely clear that additional benefits will result from acting on your suggestion, and get the listener's agreement that it is worth their while to consider the change before you move on:

'Now that I've explained that this structured approach is uniquely powerful because it is the only way to precisely match the thinking of the listener, does my suggestion make more sense to you?'

PRODUCTS VERSUS SERVICES

Customer attitudes, beliefs and therefore behaviours are different when buying services as opposed to products. It is an old adage that people love to buy, but they hate being sold to. The techniques outlined above help the potential customer to become a buyer by avoiding putting any barriers across the road to the sale. But it is arguable that although we may love to buy products where we can twiddle the knobs, admire the shiny newness of our purchase or otherwise entertain ourselves, most of us dislike buying services. A service may well solve a problem, or ineptly carried out it may cause the situation to worsen. There is nothing solid on which we may hang our expectations. Those who sell services or ideas are well advised to consider the disadvantage under which they operate and make special efforts to allow customers to buy, rather than sell.

SUMMARY

This chapter has been an attempt to write down what I usually explain and demonstrate over several days in the conference room with considerable opportunities for practice and feedback. Perhaps it will help to have a short review of the key points.

For reasons which will be plain from the next chapter, the secret of influence lies in the development of an unvarying structure once you are ready to present your ideas. This structure works for well tested and well understood psychological reasons. A short 'game plan' follows:

1. PLAN YOUR PRESENTATION FROM THE BUYER'S POINT OF VIEW

- Make your customer feel important by basing your discussion firmly on their key objective.
- Test your understanding of the most important issues or problems your listener faces. From their viewpoint, *not yours*.
- Remember that their present point of view is based on their past success and makes absolute sense to them. To change it will require compelling reasons.
- Match your mood and manner to that of your customer.

2. CREATE FOR THE CUSTOMER AN AWARENESS OF THE NEED TO ACT – NOW

When the listener confirms that your assessment of their wishes is correct:

- Demonstrate that conditions beyond the control of either of you are changing.
- Show how the changes taking place *could* cause your listener problems in the future.
- Indicate that you have the means to change potential threats to opportunities.

3. MAINTAIN AND BUILD YOUR CUSTOMER'S INTEREST

Be sure that the listener's apathy is replaced by an interest in hearing what you have to say and increase their enthusiasm:

- Mention one or two benefits which the customer will gain from using your services, products or ideas before indicating what you will do.
- Make sure they regard these as benefits and appreciate their worth.

4. TELL YOUR CUSTOMER ALL THEY NEED TO KNOW ABOUT YOUR SERVICE, PRODUCT OR IDEA

Now is your chance to paint a picture, arouse positive feelings or simply express your idea in detail. Explain in sufficient detail:

- What you offer.
- When you can supply it.
- Who else will be involved.
- What special skills and knowledge you uniquely offer.
- Key features which give assurance that the promised benefits will materialise.
- Who else, that they respect, has already successfully used your services or products.

● What they say about the experience (if you have their permission to quote them).

Link the benefits logically to prove that if one is achieved the others follow as a consequence. Show that the final benefit in your chain of logic is the listener's key objective.

5. PROVE THE BENEFITS OF YOUR SERVICES

● Stop talking.
● Wait for your customer to speak.
● Listen actively.
● Show that you have listened by repeating a key idea or feeling in your own words.
● Diffuse the emotion by showing that you understand the right of the customer to react in any way that feels right to them.
● Deal with their problem.
● Continue when you are convinced that they are satisfied and ready to listen, not before.

6. IF YOU LOSE YOUR CUSTOMER'S FAVOURABLE ATTENTION DURING THE DISCUSSION

No tricks or 'closing techniques' – *just ask*. Look for 'buying signals':

7. ASK FOR THE ORDER

● nods of agreement or approval
● building on your ideas
● willingness to give you supportive information or data

Having asked – stop talking and remain silent until you have a reply.

This method is powerful. Even more powerful is a method which, using precisely the same structure, uses questions rather than statements where appropriate. Where, through the answering of astute and relevant questions, the listener is guided toward the information with which they sell to themselves, that really is magic...

4 Mind Maps and Easy Persuasion

WHAT YOU WILL GAIN FROM THIS CHAPTER

- ● An enhanced understanding of buyer/listener psychology
- ● The concept of cognitive mapping
- ● Details of the academic and practical research which underpin the techniques described in Chapter 3

God does not give people dreams without he gives the strength to achieve them.

(Inner-city school motto)

A touch of history

In the early 1930s an organisation was formed in the United States to analyse successful sales presentations and to develop a process which would bring the customer in an unforced way toward the decision to buy. Academia took a hand, with the effect that a cognitive map of the sequence of customer thought was developed. That map (Figure 4.1) has proved its value in more than 60 years of tough practical experience and experiment. If the customer reaches satisfactory (affirmative) answers to each of the questions implied, their mind moves

TOOLS TO USE

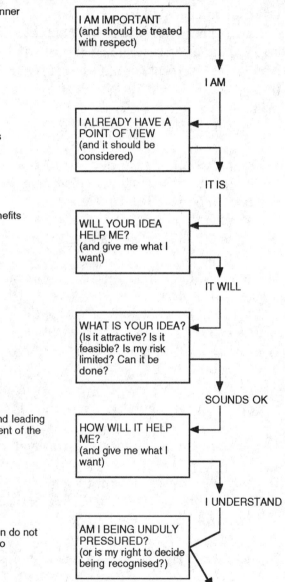

Appropriate mood and manner
Rapport building skills
Listener's key goal
Questions

I AM IMPORTANT
(and should be treated
with respect)

I AM

Questions
Current conditions
Acceptance of past actions

I ALREADY HAVE A
POINT OF VIEW
(and it should be
considered)

IT IS

One or two worthwhile benefits
Rapport

WILL YOUR IDEA
HELP ME?
(and give me what I
want)

IT WILL

Features
Skills needed
Resources available
Support and aftersales
High status users

WHAT IS YOUR IDEA?
(Is it attractive? Is it
feasible? Is my risk
limited? Can it be
done?

SOUNDS OK

Benefits logically linked and leading
unbroken to the achievement of the
listener's key goal

HOW WILL IT HELP
ME?
(and give me what I
want)

I UNDERSTAND

Avoid 'smart-alec' closes
Ask for agreement and then do not
speak again until spoken to

AM I BEING UNDULY
PRESSURED?
(or is my right to decide
being recognised?)

I AM COMFORTABLE WITH THIS
LET'S DO IT!

Figure 4.1   The path to agreement

smoothly to a positive decision. If not, you may or may not get there in the end, but the path will be long and weary. What is worse, success on one occasion will not justify the prediction of a similar outcome in the future.

The technique described in Chapter 3 is not limited in its application to sales situations, far from it. The process has been mandated for executives at the most senior level in corporations throughout the world. It works in all persuasive situations, managerial, sales and social.

Salespeople

The approach helps salespeople:

- Fully understand what leads people to buy.
- Place no barriers in the way of making the sale.
- Satisfy the immediate and long-term needs of their customers.
- Systematically analyse their sales opportunities and potential problems.
- Economically preplan their sales approach to maximise the chances of success.
- Deal confidently and effectively with the unexpected as it arises.
- Build unusual rapport by consistently communicating from the customer's point of view.
- Understand the importance of national, regional and organisational cultures and respond to them effectively.

Senior executives and managers

The approach helps senior executives and managers:

- Analyse problems and opportunities and build team and individual commitment by communicating solutions and tactics from the viewpoint of the listener.
- Test the soundness of their own and others' ideas.
- Use questions effectively to stimulate desire and action, gain information, enhance creativity and encourage involvement.
- Determine subordinates' and peers' personal goals and demonstrate how these may best be attained through the achievement of organisational objectives.
- Explain sensitive issues in a way which decreases defensiveness and develops the desire to take immediate

and effective corrective action.

- Change the behaviour of others so that in the light of the success of the new behaviours, attitudes and beliefs change in turn.
- Learn how to calm emotions and deal with difficult employees.
- Handle resistance to change.
- Get firm commitment to action from others and relax the supervisory burden.

It works widely and reliably because it is founded on a proven psychological model. I will describe in Chapter 11 how cognitive psychology differs from behaviourism. The latter insists that all that may be observed is behaviour and mental acts are at best irrelevant and at worst non-existent. Cognitive psychology insists with equal vigour that from observable behaviour mental acts may be deduced and the accuracy of that deduction may be tested by hypothesis and experiment.

To apply that thinking more simply to our case, you can analyse what people actually do when influencing the behaviour of others. Simultaneously you can examine the response of the 'buyer'. You can then deduce what is happening in the buyer's mind and develop a model. By creating a systematic response to that model of buyer behaviour you can test it and retest it in the field and in the laboratory. In science all theories remain precisely that, they are theories liable to ongoing testing and possible future challenge. Each time that they survive the test, however, the theory is strengthened. The model which drives the approach described in Chapter 3 has triumphantly survived such testing and retesting for more than 60 years. The rest of this chapter will be devoted to describing that model in detail.

Influencing behaviour is a power relationship. There is no way in the world that a power differential can be totally avoided. If I am trying to persuade you to do anything which you had not thought of doing, then my success will be dependent on the exercise of power. Buyers, whether customers, clients or subordinates, intuitively recognise this and often, in self-defence, they attempt to reverse or avoid the situation.

THE IMPORTANCE OF INDIVIDUAL INTEGRITY

Two examples may clarify what I mean. Salespeople are not generally held in high regard. The depiction of Richard Nixon as someone from whom you wouldn't buy a used car was as much an insult to used car salespeople as it was a euphemism when applied to the crooked US President. Anyone who thinks even superficially must recognise two facts.

● In our society we are all, at one time or another salespeople. I am a peddler when I put the ideas in this book to you – the fact that I am called an author is simply a specious attempt to raise my status. I am and will remain a peddler in spite of the fact that I have never worked with a label that says 'salesperson' around my neck. As a businessman, as a consultant, as an executive, writer, even as a parent, I am a salesperson.

● There is no economic activity without salespeople. The research which drives the behavioural model was born out of recognition of that fact. In the 1930s we were in the depths of what we call the 'Great Depression' – after recent experiences whether we will continue to call it that is open to doubt. Some 25 per cent of Americans had no work. That is appalling, but what is frequently not understood is that 75 per cent had jobs, and with deflation many were doing better than we sometimes realise and all were experiencing a regular increase in buying power. Those 75 out of every 100 Americans were employed largely because of the skills and performance of salespeople. As Ian Robson, the managing director of Perception Dynamics, says:

Not only are good salespeople worth their weight in gold, if you're wise you will pay them barely less than that.

All of the above notwithstanding, people fear (fear is not too strong a word) the wiles of the salesperson. They suspect that they will be swindled and that their personal integrity will be breached. This is true whether the salesperson appears in the guise of salesperson proper, consultant, boss, parent or teacher. So the first thought in the mental process of 'buying' services, products or ideas is:

I *am important and* need *to be treated with respect.*

Failure to recognise this and respond to it with sensitivity and professionalism means that the atmosphere of mutual problem solving which is essential to the development of a long-term relationship based on common interest is replaced by a fight for dominance or a flight to security. That is why we insist that the focus of the discussion is the 'buyer's' objective, and that the objective should be agreed from the start by an influencer whose mood and manner match that of the listener.

Behaviourism tells us that everything we do is to gain pleasure or to avoid pain. Our characteristic behaviour is based on a simple but powerful premise. We have tried it and for us it works. For the person doing it there is no such thing as irrational behaviour. If my normal response to opposition is to tear off my clothes and stand in the corner and scream till I'm sick, I act that way for a simple reason. I have achieved what I want by acting like that in the past. The problem is that conditions change. In my social and work life that kind of behaviour is not considered appropriate for a man in his fifties.

THE POWER OF PAST EXPERIENCE

But if you simply say, 'For God's sake grow up!', you will not change my behaviour. It is part of me. It has, to some degree, played a part in bringing me whatever success, small or great, that I have enjoyed in life. I value it as I value myself. Attack it and you attack my integrity as a human being.

If you want me to change you must show me why without threatening or damaging my sense of self-worth and self-respect. Show me that the world has changed beyond your control and outside mine, and I may see the reason to at least consider some form of change now. You are unlikely to provide me with a 'road to Damascus' experience. I will not change on the spot. But that is not your intent. What you want me to do at this stage is to listen with a more or less open mind, no more. The inescapable reasons why I should make the change that you recommend will come later.

The expression of neutral conditions and the losses which they, not my behaviour, will cause, barring me from the achievement of my objective, will do no more than sustain the favourable attention which you established earlier. They are expected to do no more. But now you have added something of great value to our relationship. I am increasingly convinced that I am dealing, not with someone who is trying to railroad me into a decision which I will regret, but with one who understands me, and more importantly understands what I am up against. I have a friend and ally.

I'M CONSIDERING CHANGE - BUT WHY YOURS?

Even if you have convinced me that the real world as it is today acts as a bar to my achieving what I want, why should I listen to your idea? Surely there are many ways to skin a cat. An hour or two of contemplation may provide me with a dozen less radical ideas than what you are about to suggest. If you have been effective in proving that today's conditions mean that my behaviour will no longer get me what I want, you will have depressed me a little. Perhaps my best immediate strategy is to retire, lick my emotional wounds, and consider the best of perhaps many ways forward.

In short, *will your idea help me and give me what I want?*

You must now show me that satisfaction of my wants is possible even in today's volatile and hostile environment. You must lead me to believe that there is something in it for me if I listen to you. More than that, you want me to listen with a positive and even an increasingly enthusiastic attitude. You must employ what the Americans call a 'helpful manner of speaking'. You must convince me that pain can be avoided and benefits can be attained.

'Don't worry, this can be avoided. You can increase sales even against tough competition and improve your profits if you...'

Now I really want to hear your idea. So tell me all and I mean *all* that is relevant to my need.

WHAT IS YOUR IDEA?

Having brought your listener this far down the mental path to compliance, they are hungry for information. What they want is facts. You would be well advised to provide them.

Now you can talk to your heart's delight. The only constraint is relevance to meeting the buyer's objective.

You can wax lyrical about the features of your product, service or idea. You can, and should, talk at length about why it will be

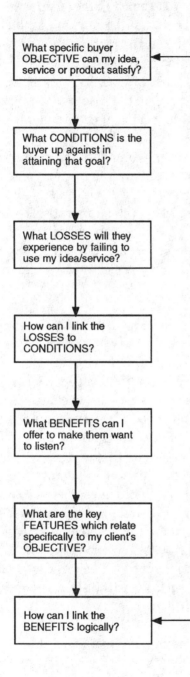

Figure 4.2   Responding to the buyer mind map

easy to implement. You can cite other users, with their permission, and report what they say about the delights of using your idea. You ought to explain about the support that you will give in implementation or your incomparable after-sales service. You can assure and reassure your listener that if they choose to use your idea they have all the resources to make it work for them. You can provide facts, figures and flights of fancy which appeal to your listener.

If you have successfully brought the listener to the point where they really want to hear what you have to say, no information is without its value. But the key information is, of course the evidence which will support the listener in inevitably achieving their key objective. Your presentation may be picturesque or even picaresque, but it must finish with a relevant feature to which you can attach a relevant benefit, because…

IT'S BENEFITS ALL THE WAY

By this stage you have a happy listener. Their normal defensiveness has been rendered unnecessary, they know that you are exclusively committed to their well-being, you have protected their self-image at every stage, you have been generous with the information they crave. Above all, you have followed a structure which is a reflection of their own mental process.

The listener's emotional need now is for the opportunity to say 'yes' with a clear conscience and a placid mind. From the last feature of your presentation must grow the final proof. That is why you now build an unbroken series of benefits, each depending logically on the one preceding it, leading unerringly to the achievement of the buyer's key objective.

The use of logic provides an unanswerable case not only for action, but for the right action, the one you recommend. But it is emotion, not logic, which makes the sale. By providing an unbroken logical chain you are:

- removing any lingering doubts
- stroking the listener's self-image by implying their grasp of reason and logic
- providing them with all the information they need to sell the idea to themselves and others

- creating the certainty that others, given the facts, will approve
- reinforcing the view that you, above all people, really understand what they want

Your job is done but you can still blow it. The buyer will suddenly have their faith in your goodwill destroyed if, at this late stage, you have an inexplicable and unjustifiable lapse of taste. Simply asking for agreement, summarising the key facts and then keeping quiet or just stopping talking will win you the 'sale'. The use of smart-alec closing techniques will lose it.

Avoid like a plague The Duke of Wellington's Revenge, the Split Decision, the Affirmative Close or any similar silliness. You have not made a sale, you have facilitated the buyer's mind in moving through a process which leads comfortably to acquiescence. Just shut up, smile and wait for them to say 'yes *please*'.

AM I BEING UNDULY PRESSURED?

SUMMARY

Cognitive science allows us to look carefully at behaviour and extrapolate what is happening in terms of mental activities. Once we have created a mind map we can test its accuracy and its general application in two ways.

First, we can say if a person thinks this, in a given situation they will behave in a particular way. Secondly, we can look at outcomes which our mind map suggests will happen only if certain things are true, and we can test to see if they are indeed true for each example we are able to identify.

Armed with our mind maps we can develop an influence technology which, properly applied, will succeed every time we effectively identify the person who has the need, resources and authority to say *yes*.

5 _Influencing through NLP_

```
┌─────────────────────────────────────────────────────┐
│         WHAT YOU WILL GAIN FROM THIS CHAPTER          │
├─────────────────────────────────────────────────────┤
│                                                       │
│  ● How to use body language positively to build      │
│    speedy and early rapport                           │
│  ● How to build excitement and enthusiasm for what    │
│    you offer                                          │
│  ● How to bring back the buyer's mood of excitement   │
│    immediately if it should wane during a long        │
│    discussion                                         │
│  ● More detail about how to speak from the listener's │
│    point of view                                      │
│  ● Why even the best of ideas fail to be accepted     │
│    and what to do to change things                    │
│                                                       │
└─────────────────────────────────────────────────────┘
```

There is only one true measure of success. To be able to do what you want to do – in your own way.

(Christopher Morley)

THERE'S NO WAY YOU CAN HIDE IT

Do you enjoy people watching? I do. If you watch a couple who are obviously in love there is a great deal of eye contact. There may be hand holding and rather more smiling than is strictly necessary, but what makes things obvious is the way their body posture and movements mirror each other exactly. However he moves, she moves. Whatever posture she adopts he adopts. If I were less of an old romantic I might be reminded of Harpo Marx pretending to be Groucho's mirror image to avoid detection as a spy in *Duck Soup*. This mirroring of behaviour clusters takes place on a much wider basis. People engaged in social discourse only need to like each other for it to occur, and that is why it is important rather than merely interesting.

Humour me if you will. The next time you are alone in a public place such as a quiet bar or park, conduct a small experiment in social psychology.

Take up a position in line of sight, but not too obviously so, of another person who is on their own. Carefully adopt a position which, without exaggeration, mirrors theirs. Sit as they do. If their legs are crossed, for example, cross your legs, right over left or left over right, to match theirs exactly. If they are upright, sit as erect as they are. If they are slumped, slump no more and no less than they.

Look carefully at the position and degree of tension in their hands and copy both with a level of care which matches your observation. Without any hint of caricature, consider the tilt of their head and their facial expression. Sunny, serious or sad, copy it as accurately as you can. As your subject moves stir yourself at a natural pace to keep your body in your best possible mirror image of theirs. Do this for several minutes.

When you feel that you are really in tune physically with the other, starting from a position which still mirrors theirs, move a limb and watch to see if they follow. If they don't, return for a while to mirroring their pose and when you feel that its appropriate try again. When they follow you, and sooner or later they will, use your power over them constructively. Straighten your posture. Lighten and brighten your expression. Hold your head comfortably high. You may be doing them more good than you will ever know.

When you are satisfied that you can control the other's movement and posture consider your own feelings.

How do you feel about the other person? Now that you can control them do you like them more? Less? Or are your feelings towards them neutral?

How do you feel about yourself? Do you feel clever? Successful? Powerful? Manipulative? Guilty? Ashamed?

Your answers to these questions are important. You have just successfully completed the first stage of building rapid and very effective rapport with another person. In doing so you have demonstrated considerable power to act on another's unconscious mind. The technology is well established, but technology is neutral. It is your decision whether you will use your skill to sell your ideas, services or products.

Always, when considering the use of a technique which is new to you, analyse your feelings and select only those which are congruent, which fit in with your value system, and which you feel good about using. It's not just ethical to approach ideas this way, it makes sound professional sense. If you doubt the validity of something you will probably do it less than well. Congruence is important too. The purpose is building long-term relationships. Long-term relationships prosper when the behaviour of both parties is internally as well as externally congruent.

If you feel, as most people do, that you now have warm, almost protective feelings toward the other person and that you have no negative feelings about yourself, you will probably regard what you have practised and learned as being a constructive skill with which you can do as much for others as you can for yourself. If your feelings, particularly about yourself, are negative, then you will choose not to use the following techniques although you may still wish to understand them. Knowledge is power, even if only defensive power.

To summarise; people who want to build exceptional rapport with others start by doing as lovers do. The sequence is always the same:

Mirroring Place your body in as close an approximation of the physical position taken by the other as is possible.

Pacing Change your position as the other changes theirs so that you mirror them in a dynamic way.

Leading Change your position independently of them. If they consistently follow you, you have:

- built exceptional feelings of personal liking and rapport towards you in the other person
- created an emotional atmosphere in which almost anything which you say or do will attract and keep their favourable attention

and you can:

● develop in the other person a mood of enthusiasm and or excitement at will

Once the other person is mirroring and pacing your movements, you can change their mood by simply and consistently expressing in speech and in body language the mood which you want them to attain. Psychiatric nurses now use this method to calm hyperactive or overemotional patients in preference to the assault of forcibly given tranquillisers.

If you choose to do this be patient – the response is by no means always immediate. Be prepared to return to mirroring the other person's posture and gestures for a while, then take the lead again. Sooner or later they will follow.

PEOPLE LIKE TO BUY FROM PEOPLE THEY LIKE

You will know by now that I use the word 'buy' loosely. If I offer you advice and you follow it, you have bought it. If I offer you my services in exchange for money and you sign a contract, you have bought, for the period of the contract at least, me, my loyalty, experience, skills and abilities, such as they are. You are more likely to buy what I peddle if you believe that I really understand your needs and, more importantly your wants. We all tend to believe that people who act as we do share our feelings and values.

Nicholas Humphries, one of the UK's most thoughtful and thought-provoking psychologists, suggests that we have developed consciousness specifically because it enables us to experience empathy. To walk a mile, as they say, in the other person's shoes.

If I am conscious of my own feelings in a situation it is possible that when I see you experiencing a similar situation I have some inkling of what positive or negative feelings you are having. If I can vicariously feel your pain my empathy will be meaningful and will cement our relationship. I can be there for you when you need someone.

Of course, it has always been argued that I cannot know what you are feeling, I can only approximate by extrapolating from my own feelings. At the very least, I empathise because I think I understand. There is some, admittedly at the moment rather thin, evidence that if I learn to use mirroring and pacing to a high degree of accuracy I can do better than that.

Consider if you will someone who is really depressed. Think about their physical posture. Their face is not so much sad as drained of all emotion, and often hard to see because their head droops. Their shoulders are bowed and they slump when they sit. Their eyes are dull, listless and unfocused. They look down or into space without any sign of interest. Although their arms may hang loosely there is often tension in their neck and shoulders. Hands may be tightly together with fingers interwoven, or one hand may pluck listlessly at the other. Where depression and anxiety coincide the legs are not merely crossed, they are intertwined and are often turned away from the body.

If you copy the pose of someone who is depressed for a few minutes it is probable that you will feel a little depressed yourself. But what if you were an expert on copying the minutiae of physical posture? You would feel very depressed. In fact you might even feel suicidal.

The interplay of mood and posture is so intimate that it is unclear whether we feel depressed because we act depressed or whether our posture is triggered by our feeling. Stand up straight. Throw out your chest and sing a jolly song. I challenge you to go on feeling miserable. So, our mood changes with our posture. So what?

The setting is a psychology laboratory. Two people sit, one either side of a glass, soundproof screen. Each has a tape recorder. The person to your left is asked to think about an experience with strong emotional connotations. They talk through the experience introspectively. That is, they don't merely describe what happened, they attempt to relive it and express verbally their thoughts and feelings. The tape recorder makes a timed record of all that is said.

The second subject, to the right of the screen, is an expert on posture/gesture modelling. They can't hear what is being said, but they can see and copy the movements of the other person's body. They too record their thoughts and feelings. The evidence is that there is a much closer similarity *between the two sets of recordings than chance or overt visual cues would permit. It's early days yet and far too early to suggest that mind reading is a possibility, but the early results are intriguing.*

There is also evidence that if you accurately copy the posture of another interesting person things start to happen. Your rate of breathing begins to be synchronised with theirs, but there's more. Your heartbeat and theirs converge. In the laboratory where it can be tested it seems that your galvanic skin response, the ability of your skin to conduct an electric current, also matches theirs, which means that your skin's dryness or dampness becomes the same as the other person as your rapport with them increases. Pupil size is the same, which, unless the level of light striking your eyes and theirs is also identical, is remarkable. With such a detailed degree of shared experience it is tantalisingly possible that shared thoughts and feelings follow.

AS I SPEAK SO I THINK — OR DO I?

There is no need to limit your rapport building to body language. I believe that spoken and written language has a magic of its own. Practitioners of neurolinguistic programming (NLP) believe that the words we use clearly indicate our preferred thinking style. There is little doubt that although we all think sometimes in words, sometimes in visual images and sometimes by conjuring up feelings, emotional and physical, for many of us a single style of thought is easier and more 'natural'.

I think in spoken words. There is a persistent chatter in my head. I find it somewhat difficult to visualise with any clarity and close to impossible to think in terms of physical feelings.

When I am training people and it is relevant to what we are discussing, I sometimes point to an empty chair and ask them to mentally place someone in the chair so that they can see them clearly. On average roughly a third of people tell me that they are able to see an imagined being sitting in the physical chair. A further third report that they transpose chair and occupant to their heads and see both there clearly while the real chair remains empty. The rest, including me, are only able at best to

GENERIC

I understand you

I want to communicate
something to you

Do you understand what
I'm trying to
communicate?

I know that to be true

I'm not sure about that

I don't like what you're
doing

Life is great

VISUAL

I see your point

I want you to take a look
at this

Do you see what I
mean?

Beyond a shadow of a
doubt

It's pretty hazy to me

I take a dim view of it

Things are sparkling

AUDITORY

I hear what you are
saying

I want to make this loud
and clear

Does it sound right to
you?

It's accurate, word for
word

It just doesn't sound right

I don't like the sound of
that

Life is in harmony

KINAESTHETIC

I am in touch with your
ideas

I want you to get a grasp
on this

Can you get hold of this?

The information is as
solid as a rock

It feels wrong to me

It just doesn't feel right

*Everything is warm and
wonderful*

Figure 5.1   Representational systems

produce fleeting visions apparently somewhere between our ears.

I then ask the group to imagine the feel of stroking a kitten and subsequently invite them to change to handling a peach. On one occasion a young lady in the group when imagining stroking the kitten had a bout of violent sneezing. She assured me that she was allergic to cats.

NLP claims that as we think, so we speak. So if I were to ask you to 'show me the whole picture so that I can see it from your perspective' I would be asking you to paint me a word picture or better yet actually draw me a diagram, because that is how I am indicating that I find it easiest to think. Similarly, if I were to say 'I don't quite grasp that, help me to get a handle on it', I would be indicating that I would more readily understand your idea if you expressed it in terms of feeling, in this case physical feeling. A list of these 'predicates' or representational systems is given in Figure 5.1.

To build even stronger rapport it is suggested that the response should be in the same language – visual begetting visual, kinaesthetic (feeling) promoting kinaesthetic, and auditory (words) responded to with auditory.

Look for a moment at the list of predicates in Figure 5.1. Do you share my feeling that they are basically clichés with which we all tend to pepper our speech? If this is the case, then we get the best of both worlds. If NLP can be relied on we can match predicates and powerfully build rapport; if not, we can match away and no harm done. No one will find it odd if we use clichés.

Some specialists claim that not only the words we use but also the way we say them betrays our preferred thinking style. Tony Robbins claims that visual thinkers speak quickly as they flick through the pictures in their heads. Kinaesthetics, on the other hand, speak very slowly, with deep intakes and exhalations of breath punctuating the words. Auditories speak fairly slowly with silent pauses while they search for the right words.

WE SOUND AS WE THINK

We can deepen rapport by listening to and matching:

● **Volume** – the relative loudness or quietness of the other's voice

- **Tempo** – the speed of speech, slow, fast, drawled, staccato
- **Rhythm** – the combination of patterns and speed which causes the voice to lilt or to remain steady
- **Tone** – a combination of pitch and style: high, low, harsh, soft

If you note a slight reservation in the way I have written the above few paragraphs, let me come clean. Recent research suggests that there is no necessary relationship between thinking style and the use of predicates. Because they are clichés most of the predicates listed may be popular in a given culture at a given time, and they may not indicate anything about how any particular individual thinks.

That notwithstanding, it has been known for many years in organisational psychology and group dynamics that the use of a 'common language' enhances bonding within teams. It seems to work for me and many others – try it.

However, it's easy to imagine that others really are like us. Elias Porter did some research in the 1970s which suggested that our deepest hurts and greatest hatreds are reserved for those we most deeply love, who turn out to be a little less like us than we thought in matters which we feel to be important. Be careful, therefore, how you handle rapport. If the reality is that you cannot be entirely sincere, be, at the very least, consistent.

THOSE OLD METAPROGRAMS

As I explained in Chapter 4, more than 60 years' research has been committed to analysing success. Some thought has also been given to the sources of failure.

Someone buys an idea, a product or a service because the benefits which are promised 'press their hot button'. So why is it that I can offer you benefits which would have me turning cartwheels, the benefits can be in an unbroken logical chain leading to the achievement of an agreed desired objective – and you still say 'no thank you'? One reason is the most obvious and probably the most likely: I am not you and you are not me.

Suppose you and I agree that you want to make a million. I show you a novel route full of excitement, risk and challenge when you are a person who clings to the well tried formula, calm, unstretching and, above all, risk free. Will you buy? Will camels fly unaided?

When I talked of presenting an idea from the listener's point of view, I meant from the listener's point of view in every foreseeable detail.

The business of deciding which of the many benefits an idea offers will turn me on is relatively easy, in the sense that those which lead logically to the attainment of my heart's desire are those which are relevant. The difficult part is that if I don't like the sound of the journey I won't buy.

Can psychology help here? You will not be surprised to know that it can. Research suggests that the types of benefits which are likely to woo can be identified by dividing the population into four of eight trait types.

Approachers are people who regard the shortest distance between two points to be the most challenging. Offer them a hint of challenge and they gallop off with lance at the tilt. *Retreaters* seek the route of least risk. Their preference is for no risk at all, but if risk there must be your influencing strategy must specify precisely how it is to be minimised. Offer an approacher a retreater's set of benefits and they will be contemptuous. Suggest to a retreater a list of benefits which would send an approacher over the top, all guns blazing, and they will cower in the bottom of the trench until they can be sure that you have gone away and left them in peace. I would like to believe that I am an approacher, but I don't want to risk finding out!

APPROACHERS VERSUS RETREATERS

Have you ever noticed that if you ask some people to comment on two things there are some who immediately identify those things which are similar about them? Such people are *matchers*. To make them want what you have to offer, point out all the similarities between this and something they have told you they have successfully done or used before. *Mismatchers*, on the other hand, look for differences. Show them how your new idea is unique and you have their interest.

MATCHERS VERSUS MISMATCHERS

Some of us don't give a hang what the world thinks. As long as we feel good about any outcome that is what counts. To

INTERNAL VERSUS EXTERNAL

persuade such people we need to emphasise the good feelings they will experience and understate or ignore what others might say. Conversely, some pay great heed to what the world and his wife think has merit. With them, the turn-on comes from knowing that the world will think well of them.

An excellent, but extreme example of one who relies on *external* frames of reference is Socrates who, wrongly condemned, refused to escape from imprisonment because he believed that in a well ordered state it was more proper for an innocent man to die than to bring disrepute on authorites who were doing their best to maintain order in difficult circumstances. To appeal to one who goes by external frames of reference your idea and the benefits it offers must be aligned with the perceived rules, explicit and implied, of society, family or organisation.

SORTING BY SELF VERSUS SORTING BY OTHERS

There have long been arguments between sociobiologists as to whether altruism, putting other's needs before your own, could have evolved in a species history in which the 'fittest' go on to breed and thus to have their line survive. This is an arrid argument. We are the results of evolution. Altruism does exist. Therefore altruism has, or has had, competitive value.

Some of us are *selfish* and put our own wants and needs constantly before others. Others are more concerned with the well-being of the *group*, whether it be large or small.

The first group seek benefits which are specifically for them personally. They have relatively little interest in the general good. Identify such people and stress the direct benefits which they will experience.

Those who put the general good first are easier to recognise than you might think. Those who day by day demonstrate their supportive and sometimes self-sacrificing behaviour have been shown in psychological assessment to use similar behaviours in one-on-one contacts. They give more eye contact, they show agreement by more nodding and supportive gestures or comments. Look carefully for these cues and respond to them by emphasising group, community, national or even global benefits.

Beware, however, of those who say they put others first. Their egocentricity is usually betrayed by their inclination to expound on other people's lack of gratitude.

It would be a strangely uncommitted world if you didn't have strong preferences among the motivations and behaviours which I have summarised. But always remember that in influencing the behaviour of others we deal with the world as it is, not as we wish it to be. Our starting point is to accept people as they are right now and select the tools of influence accordingly. Our goal may be to change the world, but, as with any worthwhile strategic plan, having decided where we want to go we assess coolly and honestly where we are right now and develop our tactics accordingly.

OK, I'VE BUILT RAPPORT – WHAT IF I LOSE?

The SARAH technique described in Chapter 3 is the ideal way to use words and actions to satisfy the emotional and rational needs of the less than happy listener. However, there is a simpler way to return the once enthusiastic and now neutral listener to their previous excited state. It is called 'anchoring'.

You have been explaining your idea for protecting the Menai Bridge from rust by boiling it in wine. For most of the time I have been wildly enthusiastic. I am certainly not anti now, but my eyes have glazed over just a little and you fear that I am losing that old 'let's do it' look. If you anchored my previous state of peak excitement you have no problem. Anchoring works like this.

As we talk you watch and listen to me carefully. Possibly by mirroring, pacing and leading you move me to a point of extreme enthusiasm for the idea. When my words, body language and gestures indicate that I am at a level of excitement which is unlikely to be exceeded, you, sharing my enthusiasm, touch my arm or perhaps tap your pencil sharply on the table as if to emphasise our excitement. If, at a later stage, I seem to go off the boil you can return me to my former state by exactly repeating the touch, or if you used a sound, producing exactly the same sound again.

The keys to anchoring successfully are as follows.

The more intense the state the easier it is to anchor. If you choose to anchor enthusiasm wait until I'm on a real high. You will know by changes in my breathing, eye movements,

The intensity of the state

engorgement of my lower lip with increased blood flow, my posture, muscle tone, pupil dilation, skin colour and reflectiveness and my voice, particularly pace and volume.

Uniqueness of the stimulus

If you are an uncontrolled and uncontrollable pencil tapper, don't expect another tap of your pencil to be effective. Similarly, if you are coughing and spluttering a single voluntary cough won't do it. At a party where everybody's conversational style is to place their hand on the shoulder of their listener, a touch on the shoulder will not work. A touch or sound are ideal anchorers, but they must be unique in the context in which they are used.

Accuracy of stimulus reproduction

The more accurate the replication of the stimulus – the location and pressure of a touch, the volume, pitch and tone of a sound – the more effective anchoring will be.

SUMMARY

This chapter has carefully picked from the many claims made for NLP those which have been validated by research rather than by experience or anecdote. That is not to say that other ideas from NLP are to be dismissed. Keep an open mind. Read some of the plethora of excellent books on the subject. Conduct your own experiments and use what works for you.

Another idea from Tony Robbins. When you make any change in your behaviour, subject the change to an ecological check. Be satisfied that neither you nor those around you will be damaged by what you propose.

The Power of the Word 6

```
WHAT YOU WILL GAIN FROM THIS CHAPTER
```

- An understanding of why verbal language is at least as important as body language (regardless of what some academics may claim)
- Some thoughts on verbal language as the cement of social interaction
- Examples of words to be avoided
- Examples of words to be used
- Some brief thoughts on style

Language is for varied life – and when distinct forms of personal relationship are possible – not for exchanging standard information units among standard users.

(Mary Midgley)

Verbal language is important to humanity. When we are alone, whether we believe it to be an early sign of madness or not, we talk to ourselves. We talk to our plants and pets. As babies we babble long before we have words with which to express ourselves and research shows that the happiest babies babble

IT'S AS MUCH WHAT YOU SAY AS THE WAY THAT YOU SAY IT

most. Twenty years or so ago when sensory deprivation experiments were a popular area of scientific study, it was noticed that people deprived of stimulation talked or sang incessantly to themselves.

Much of our social language serves no informative purpose. We swap clichés and burbles at parties with little intent other than to create strong or transient social bonds with others. Robin Dunbar of the University of Liverpool suggests that we use talk as our primate cousins use grooming. But, if we want to show the world how clever, caring, witty or concerned we are, language, including body language, is all that we have. And in many situations an important part of that is talk.

Language is and always has been magical. I don't mean that in some whimsical way, I mean it literally. Language is the structure and the key tool of magic. If you feel inclined to put a spell on someone, to change them perhaps into a bat or a bobalink, what do you do? You recite something. An incantation may or may not do the trick, but what is clear is that language works when behavioural change is what you desire.

IMPOVERISHED EXCESS

It seems that almost every word of any importance has been used, and often overused, to sell something. Advertising copywriters and spin doctors have squeezed the guts out of language and left its remnants weakened and debased. Words such as 'mega', 'great', 'outstanding' now mean little more than 'good'. As a result, would-be influencers tend too often to qualify what they are saying. The word 'quite' creeps into conversation as we are told that something is 'quite useful' or 'quite good'. Just as strong words should not be overused, weak words, or words which sap the strength of others, should be avoided altogether.

In advertising they differentiate between tombstone and haemorrhoid advertising. Tombstone refers to the beautiful and expensive advertisements designed to support brand image. They usually run for short periods, to be overtaken by a new and usually even more beautiful and expensive campaign.

Haemorrhoid advertisements don't use pictures, they depend entirely on words. Their message is simple: if you have a pain in the butt we have the analgesic for you. They run for ever because until you are a sufferer from the pain which they claim to cure you don't bother to read them. Glamour catches the eye, but is transient. Well directed use of language sells and goes on selling.

It is tautologous to suggest that the written word must be dependent on language, but is it equally necessary to choose spoken language with care? Great orators have always thought so. Abraham Lincoln is invested by mythology with having scrawled the Gettysburg Address on the equivalent of the back of a cigarette packet, but no word of it is redundant, none fails to play a specific role in creating the desired effect.

At the other political extreme, Adolf Hitler was a brilliant orator. He was a master of the 'rule of three' which is taught on virtually every public speaking course. The rule is not satisfied by simply finding three things to say. The power lies in repetition of a key word and the rhythm of the whole phrase.

WORN-OUT WORDS

Some years ago a corporation in which I worked decided to introduce job performance appraisal by committee. Groups of senior executives would sit around a table and express their views about an individual. These views were discussed, some kind of consensus was eventually reached and the appropriate boxes were ticked on the form.

A middle manager's work was being appraised. In general, those that had spoken about him had expressed the view that he was creative, firm, consistent and courageous in promoting both his decisions and his strongly held values. A senior executive of the Personnel Department spoke next. He had jotted down a series of words and read them with evident satisfaction.

'I find him intransigent, prototypal, opinionated and disputatious in the extreme.'

All hell broke loose. Those who had already spoken and those who were yet to speak were united in their attack on the hitherto smug personnel manager. There was an immediate assault on the Personnel Department and all its crazy schemes, including meaningless box ticking and time-wasting appraisal by committee. As the personnel manager sought to defend his department, old scores were brought out and lovingly dusted prior to being settled. Hidden agendas became the primary purpose of the meeting. The row neatly filled the better part of what had promised to be a rather uneventful afternoon, dislocated the appraisal schedule and caused simmering resentments which probably linger still in some breasts.

The irony is that the group around the table were unanimous in their good opinion of the manager being appraised. The personnel manager also meant that the subject was 'creative, of sound judgement, logical in presenting and firm in defending his views.' Feeling threatened by his relative lack of formal education, he had sought the most impressive words he could find. Sadly, his thesaurus had let him down.

Weak and overused words

The Plain English Society very properly draws attention to overused and therefore weak words. Some are overused because they are used, as our personnel manager intended, to impress. They don't. They ofen confuse or put off the listener or reader. But how seductive their charms are.

Some examples of overused words might include:

- ambience
- continuum
- interaction
- interfacing
- marginalise
- synergy

Nothing is wrong with any of these words if their meaning is precise, unable to be expressed more simply and clearly to the receiver. But that is not how they are generally used. They become a jargon which, after it has gained general acceptance among some in-crowd, is used indiscriminately to bolster a weak argument.

Other weak words are used so frequently that they spread like treacle and lose their original clarity and power:

- amazing
- fantastic
- meaningful
- nice
- pretty
- terrific

New and forceful expressions enter the language from time to time. They are fun to use, and are often powerfully expressive while they are fresh. When they have been overused they make speech and writing stale, predictable and either boring, irritating or both.

Do you enjoy reading or hearing:

- at the end of the day
- making the best of a bad job
- cold hard facts
- take on board
- back at the ranch
- walk your talk
- down to the nitty gritty

Wasting words weakens language and its power to communicate. Why write 'at a later date' when 'later' is all that is needed? Is 'in relation to' in any way an improvement on 'about'? Is something which is 'completely useless' in some wonderful way more useless than 'useless'? If you will be 'very pleased' with the results of putting the ideas of this book into practice, might it not give you a stronger motive to read and adopt them if I told you that you will be 'delighted'?

Passive expressions are weak and sometimes confusing.

Passive and negative

- The doctor saw the patient
- The patient was seen by the doctor

and

- The doctor was seen by the patient

may have the same meaning, or they may not. 'The doctor examined the patient' is clear and simple.

Similarly, negative expressions have been shown to be more difficult to understand than positive alternatives.

Confusibles

English is a rich language because no two words have precisely the same meaning. Are you sure that you know the difference between:

- amiable and amicable
- classic and classical
- continual and continuous
- credible and creditable
- disinterested and uninterested

Brevity

Brevity may be the soul of wit, but is it always desirable in writing or speech? It shows that you have thought carefully about what you need to communicate and have pruned redundancies and repetitions. If the best way to get your idea across is in brief, that is fine, but concise is not always best. Style is important in building the relationship between receiver and sender. Many readers will tolerate a certain amount of wandering if through it they come to feel that they know the author. And, as I have explained, those who are really interested in an idea, product or service and are trying to decide what to do like to have as much information as possible. As we say when training sales people: 'When customers want to know, they really want to know.' There are times when more is better.

THE PSYCHOLOGY OF LANGUAGE

Psycholinguistics has become a major area of psychological study. The belief is that language is so critical to what makes us human that it is worthy of the most detailed study. Language is so important, in evolutionary terms, that it makes our brains lopsided. In 95 per cent of human brains the areas for language acquisition and use are on the left side close to the temple. This area is larger in 65 per cent of brains than the corresponding part of the right hemisphere, so rich are the cells and their connections devoted to language.

Most psychologists believe that language is so rich, and the number of possible combinations of words is so variable, that there is no theory of learning which can fully explain how we acquire and use language. Even a small child with a limited vocabulary can produce and understand a range of verbal statements far exceeding the number of seconds in a human life span. That would mean, as Noam Chomsky claims, that we have an innate predisposition to acquire language. This idea that we are born prewired to learn our mother tongue is further reinforced by research which suggests that if this predisposition is not applied before the end of puberty, normal language development becomes impossible.

All higher animals, particularly all mammals, communicate. Signs, signals, sounds and smells are part of the communication portfolio. But language as we know it is our inheritance alone. No other animal can truly talk or write. Further, there is no such thing as a simple human language. Any language of any human group is sufficiently sophisticated to enable the expression of the most subtle abstract thought. This has led some behavioural scientists to suggest that the use of language to convince or be convinced is also species specific and innate.

Experiments with identical twins who have been separated soon after birth indicate that primary mental abilities, perceptual and motor skills have the strongest basis in hereditary, personality traits much less so. The interplay of hereditary and culture is such that we may be hardwired to respond to language, but the specifics of how we choose to use it are culture dependent. Our culture puts a high value on leadership and influence. Language is a key tool of both.

POWER WORDS

Let us consider some practical research carried out for a practical purpose. John Caples, a professional and very successful copywriter, knew which ads sold. What he was keen to know was whether there was a magic word or words which 'hit the hot button' of the buyer every time? A count against 100 headlines of advertisements which had the desired effect left little doubt. The word most often used was *you*. For confirmation, the second most common word was *your*.

If you are looking for the magic word of influence then the facts have a double message. 'You' is the power word of all power words. Further, it is the one word which can never be overused or devalued. Putting the listener or reader at the centre of the communication and keeping them there is an important key to success.

In some circumstances numbers actually speak louder than words. Imagine I am selling a book or perhaps, just to make the whole thing nicely circular, a sales training seminar. Which do you think would be the biggest draw:

● Learn the secrets of…

or

● Learn the 11 secrets of…?

The number works every time. Among other reasons, most people reading maybe able to shrug off the first statement with 'I know the secrets of…' The second approach, however, challenges them to test their memory for all 11. With the best will and the best brain in the world few, if any, would be able to reel off 11 secrets of anything on demand. If they think they need or want to be able to – they're sold.

These ideas have been donated to the world by the advertisers of *Readers' Digest* and copied by compliance professionals of every kind, including the greats like David Ogilvie. Like or loathe *Readers' Digest*, it has a proud history of influencing buying decisions without which it would not be a global bestseller. The key words of its offerings have been:

● A new…
● How to…
● The 15 secrets of…
● Science shows that…
● 10 ways to…
● How can you…
● Your personal guide to…
● Should you…
● The sure fire way to…
● 6 steps to…
● Are you…
● Why…

Wider research has indicated that other words which have the power to move the decision-making process forward include 'good', 'discover', 'money', 'easy', 'guaranteed' and 'health'.

Language has the power to move – in every sense of that

word, from rabble-rousing to the tear in the eye. Never underestimate the power of words. Faith may indeed move mountains, but words move people.

SUMMARY

Psychologists have caused considerable confusion about the power of words. Too many books on non-verbal communication give the false impression that words and their meaning don't count. The reason for this is, I suspect, simple.

Research into non-verbals has hinged on an observer's ability to guess what is the communicative intent of a speaker either using mime or nonsense syllables. Success in extrapolating meaning from such pantomimes has been cited as indicating the relative importance of posture, gesture, tone of voice etc. So far so good – all of those things are important in transfering meaning from one person to another. Only words, however, have the power to bring precision into the communication process. Anyone doubting this should seek out and watch carefully film of the late Milton Erickson hypnotising a subject with simple words alone. That is an object lesson in the use of language to influence behaviour.

Think about and use strong words, recognise which words are powerful persuaders, and do your personal best to improve the general level of style in speech and in writing.

7   *Motivation is Always the Key*

WHAT YOU WILL GAIN FROM THIS CHAPTER

- Behaviour is always motivated
- Identify the motive and you understand the behaviour
- Satisfy the motive and you manage the behaviour
- What Maslow really meant by 'self-actualising'

A man whose only tool is a hammer tends to treat everything as a nail.

(Abraham Maslow)

MOTIVES, PERSONALITY AND BEHAVIOUR

Psychology teaches us that needs and motivation drive behaviour. Obnoxious or unacceptable behaviour results from a misdirected attempt to satisfy motives which are deeply held. To the degree that a theory of 'personality' has any meaning at all, it is in terms of the very different needs which drive you or me to behave as we do.

Understand my needs from my observable behaviour, help me to satisfy them and direct my attention to the potential satisfaction of 'higher', less potent but more liberating needs and you will be successful in changing my behaviour.

Since all theories of motivation are at base interchangeable I will concentrate on what for most is the 'daddy', and probably least understood, of them all – that of Abraham Maslow.

To really understand Maslow's approach and to avoid either under- or overvaluing his work, you need to know a little about how science works and how Maslow in particular worked. Maslow, like Einstein, was a creative scientist, a dreamer and a conductor of 'thought experiments'. Such scientists take their knowledge of the world and the way it appears to work and design a theory. A theory makes no claim to be true. It claims only to be credible or plausible and useful. When the theory is sufficiently plausible it is tested to establish whether it is useful.

To test a theory, the laboratory scientist starts from a hypothesis. A hypothesis is a logical deduction that if a theory is true, something which is testable may be observed. If the hypothesis, which can, unlike a theory, be demonstrated to be true or false, is shown to be true in practice, the theory is supported and therefore useful in that we are able to make accurate predictions from it. Similarly, a theory is weakened if a hypothesis which is a logical deduction from it turns out to be false in experience. Maslow's theory, therefore, is neither true nor false – but it is useful.

First Maslow tells us the assumption on which his theory is based:

Man is a wanting animal – and what he wants is more.

He claims two things from this statement. First, it is in the nature of humans to be driven by their needs and desires. Secondly, that those needs and desires evolve over time in a way that is specific and predictable. Thus we are able to show a hierarchy or ladder of needs up which we climb through life (Figure 7.1).

That is not to say that we experience our needs one at a time in some form of quantum which must be fulfilled in total before we are free to pass on to higher things. Rather, we experience a range of needs simultaneously, with our ability to move to the higher rungs of the ladder dependent on the degree to which the lower needs have been satisfied and how strong our individual needs are.

Need	Definition	Results of denial
INTERNAL FRAMES OF REFERENCE – NEED TO CONTRIBUTE FOR SELF		
Self-actualisation	The need to continuously develop in ways which are personally important to the individual.	Feelings of futility, alienation, bitterness, wasted chances, being in a rut, hopelessness.
	To feel that one is fully using personal resources to become all that one is capable of becoming.	Possibly depression or anxiety neurosis.
Cognitive autonomy	The need to be proactively understanding and acting on the environment.	Frustration, a sense of being exploited. Resentment at not finding or being given opportunities.
	Taking personal responsibility. Not being coerced or manipulated. In control of one's life and work.	Chronic and growing anxiety, despair.
Aesthetic autonomy	The need to create and have psychological ownership of something of beauty and uniqueness.	Withdrawal, focus on activities outside the workplace.
	Making a significant contribution. Encapsulated in the expression 'planting a shade tree for others to sit under'.	Frustration and a growing sense of the pointlessness of work.
EXTERNAL FRAMES OF REFERENCE – NEED TO CONTRIBUTE IN TEAMS		
Esteem/status	The need for recognition and prestige. The basis of self-respect. Knowing that we count for something.	Loss of confidence creating a poor self-image, self-doubt, shame. A feeling of being an undeserved victim.
Social	The need to be a valued member of a group. The confirmation that others find us likeable.	Loneliness, withdrawal, feelings of low self-worth and insecurity. Sometimes a need to hit back.
Security	The need to know that our world is stable and predictable. Confidence that gains made can be conserved.	Tension, anxiety, fear, panic, self-absorption.
ENFORCED SELF-ABSORPTION		
Physiological	The requirements of healthy functioning of the body and continuance of the species.	Pain, physical discomfort, illness, even death.

(Left margin: Need strength ↓; Right margin: Maturity ↑)

Figure 7.1   Making more of Maslow

Maslow regards the lower needs, those which are essential to survival of the individual and the species, to be stronger since if they are threatened we will concentrate on them to the exclusion of all else.

Maslow's theory explains why unsatisfied needs tend to make behaviour increasingly unacceptable. Behaviour moves from unpleasant to totally obnoxious as needs are perceived as being threatened or thwarted. The frustration of needs is serious, as can be seen from the figure.

If we understand the needs of others, we can manipulate the situation so that these needs are in part met through interaction with us. In this way behaviour improves to the degree where a rational exchange can take place. Please note that I speak of manipulating the *situation* not the person – the difference is critical.

Behaviour can be ameliorated by removing the sense of threat to needs and can ultimately be guided to that of those who are at the highest positions on the needs hierarchy. What Maslow called self-actualisation is focused on the individual, but is the ultimate in socialisation. Those who are at the highest levels on Maslow's famous triangle are driven by a need to build constructive relationships of appropriate warmth aimed at mutual success.

The self-actualising individual is the ideal person with whom to work. We all have the power to move people through Maslow's hierarchy of needs by ensuring that lower needs are met. The self-actualiser is an ideal, but given skill, knowledge and commitment, we have the power to help create that ideal. We must, of course, understand what we are trying to do and why we are doing it. Let's start with the goal, then we will analyse the problems and the means.

THE SELF-ACTUALISING PERSON

We have a hidden agenda to help each difficult person to move smoothly and easily to the behaviour typical of a self-actualising person. With that in mind, perhaps we ought examine just what Maslow meant by the expression 'self-actualising'.

CHARACTERISTICS OF THE SELF-ACTUALISING PERSON

Efficient perception of reality

Maslow claimed and research has confirmed that self-actualisers are able consistently to make accurate judgements about themselves and others. They are prone neither to arrogance nor undue humility in their assessment of themselves and their own behaviour, and are more easily able to detect 'the spurious, the fake and the dishonest' in others. Since they are motivated to achieve quality outcomes, they are liable to make their judgements of others clear to them. They are outspoken in their demand not to have their time wasted. If you wish to influence the behaviour of another, these are undoubtedly characteristics which you should and will welcome. Time-wasters and easy dupes are equally problematic to the ethical influencer.

Acceptance

There is a prayer that God should give us:

the ability to change what should be and can be changed, to endure what cannot be changed, and to recognise the difference.

The self-actualiser has been blessed with a greater than normal ability to recognise the realities of life and to avoid wasting effort trying to change the unchangeable. Sometimes the unavoidable has high emotional overtones, such as the death of a loved one. In such situations the acceptance of what cannot be changed is sometimes misinterpreted by those who are more emotional or more unrealistic as a lack of feeling. Clear-sightedness about what cannot be changed is often accompanied by a desire to change what can and should be transformed.

Freshness of appreciation

The beauty of the world is appreciated 'again and again, freshly and naively' by the self-actualiser. The ten thousandth lovely sunset or exquisite flower can evoke the same awestruck and joyous response as the first. What is true of the beauties of nature is true also of the beauties of argument. The concise, rational and complete argument has a beauty all its own. Thus the scientist or mathematician is prone to accept a theory or theorem for its beauty before formal proof is completed. Einstein, Dirac and Feynmann are among the many great scientists who have seen the truth of an unproved theorem because of its beauty and equally have recognised the falsity of a plausible mathematical idea purely because it was 'ugly'.

Spontaneity

The self-actualiser tends to behave spontaneously, but is simple, natural and logical rather than eccentric or merely unconventional. For many the lyrical word 'spontaneous' could be replaced by the more practical 'decisive'. When convinced, the self-actualising person seeks, in Churchill's phrase, 'action this day'.

Solution centred

The self-actualiser is clear on goals and sees problems very much as a challenge to be resolved and not as a means of apportioning blame. Ethical questions are often of great importance to these people, who avoid pettiness in thought as well as deed. Their interests tend to be global and their

timeframes of long duration. There is no tendency in the self-
actualising person to have a childish demand for benefits now,
effort later.

Although clear on outcomes, self-actualisers are determined
that every step of the journey should have value. It is not
enough to do the right thing. They demand of themselves that
they do the right thing the right way at the right time.

*The journey is the
goal*

By avoiding undue emotional involvement in issues, the self-
actualiser is able to concentrate to an abnormal degree on
getting things done. They are happy with their own company
and can work as effectively alone as within a team. If you want to
create and sustain your own miracles of achievement, develop
and foster the self-actualisers in your team.

Detachment

Self-actualising people can steer clear of becoming prisoners
of their culture or environment. They tend to have a very low
need for the approval of others and can swim against the tide if
their judgement is that it is flowing in the wrong direction. They
are not, however, 'rebels without a cause'. To them the cause is
what drives the behaviour and the cause must be a just one.

*Independence from
culture and
environment*

Research shows that self-actualising individuals will be good
team players for as long as the team pursues goals which are
seen by them as appropriate. But they are resistant to any idea
that things must be done in a given way because 'that is the way
that we've always done it around here'. In large organisations
self-actualisers are often seen as 'making waves' and are too true
to their values to play the political game of reaching the top first
and creating change after. Bureaucracy, national or corporate, is
inimical to self-actualisation.

*Confidence in their
individuality*

Self-actualisers demonstrate a strong urge to be of service to
mankind. They tend, however, to reject the easy route and seek
to do something revolutionary and meaningful. Their concern for
people does not by any means make them easy to get along
with. They demand a great deal of themselves and others and
are readily moved to anger or disgust with those whose
principles are elastic.

*Desire to be of
service*

Democratic on principle, there is a constant and considerable
danger that the need for quality of outcome drives the self-
actualiser to be autocratic in practice. Like Winston Churchill,
self-actualising individuals know of no better political system

Democratic

than democracy. Like Maslow, they believe in the ultimate perfectibility of the human animal. Like you and me, perhaps, they experience practical qualms about putting decision making into the hands of the mob.

Interpersonal relationships

Self-actualisers seek to develop deep interpersonal relationships with few others rather than have more superficial ties with many. If you create a bond with a self-actualising individual it will have to be for life, but only if you continue to work at it.

Humour

The self-actualising individual is typically one who laughs with rather than at others. There is a tendency to enjoy jokes about the shortcomings of humanity in general rather than any perceived 'inferiority' of an individual. If anyone enjoys racist, sexist or 'off-colour' humour it is certain that their tendency toward self-actualisation is limited or non-existent. The old style salesman's repertoire of dirty jokes is not a high road to a relationship. This is not to say that the self-actualiser is a prig – the jokes must just be relevant and of high quality.

Creativeness

Maslow and his experimenters found that without exception self-actualisers are inventive and original. They respect and value the ideas of others, but their creativity leads them to seek novel and improved ways of using concepts and ideas. Show them a better way which is novel, attractive and feasible, and they will be your advocates to the world.

Peak experiences

Research also suggests that self-actualising people have more peak experiences than most of us. A peak experience is the sense of oneness with one's surroundings which, at the same time, creates a sense of unlimited power and joy allied with humility and feelings of deep concern for the whole of creation. Self-actualisers are, however, seldom religious in the accepted sense of the word. They respond to the magic of nature, the formal beauty of argument and the warmth of a relationship with unusual delight, but they retain the right to enquire.

The relatively frequent peak experience makes self-actualisers the ideal subject for anchoring (see Chapter 5).

SUMMARY

All behaviour is motivated. Motives which are frustrated are a primary source of unacceptable behaviour.

The characteristics of the self-actualising individual have been studied, carefully documented and are given here as a description of the ideal person whoose behaviour we might wish to influence. We can help others to move toward a state of self-actualisation, and the technology to do this is the theme of the following chapter.

Since the greatest challenge is the most worthwhile, Chapter 8 concentrates on how to change the behaviour of the most difficult people...

8 *Dealing with Difficult People*

WHAT YOU WILL GAIN FROM THIS CHAPTER

- How to change the behaviour of difficult people and make them open to influence
- How to focus those who are subject to diversion back onto the agreed action – and help them deliver.

Nil illegitimum carborundum

(Schoolboy dog Latin tag)

Why bastard? Wherefore base?

(William Shakespeare, *King Lear*)

Psychometrics seeks to measure behaviour or personality traits. It often does so by taking simple measurements which place individuals on a straight line continuum. For example:

HOSTILE _____ x _____ WARM

suggests that the subject x is somewhat more warm than hostile, but is close enough to the middle position to be verging on neutral. The problem with this one-dimensional form of measurement is that many very different individuals would score the same on a single continuum. With only one measurement:

● information is limited
● different can appear to be the same
● similar also appears to be the same and there is no obvious way of identifying which is which

Kaiser and Koffey, two psychologists who flourished in the first half of the twentieth century, sought a solution to these problems. This was to take two measurements and put the scales at right angles to each other. That way, instead of a straight line with a limited number of points we have a plane with each individual assigned to a unique position among an infinity of points (Figure 8.1).

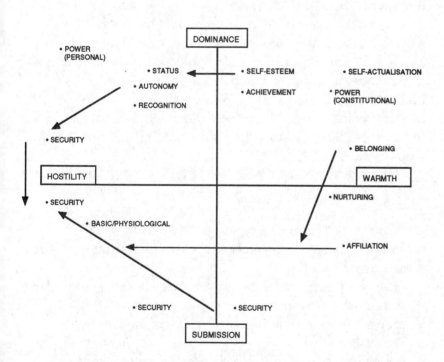

Arrows indicate probable movement when motivational needs are threatened or denied.
Satisfaction moves behaviour to upper right quadrant.

Figure 8.1   Motivators of unacceptable behaviour

As it happens Kaiser and Koffey chose to use two scales:

- dominance to submissiveness
- hostility to warmth

which are of particular value when considering the behaviour of 'difficult' people.

What makes a person behave badly is not some genetic predisposition to be difficult. It is almost always a chosen tactic which from their current perception seems to offer the best chance of fulfilling a need. Even very self-destructive behaviours result from the individual either having found them to work in the past (like somebody who 'childishly' carries forward the tantrums which worked so well in the nursery into adult life), or they are used because the individual knows of nothing better.

When we behave badly most of us are being negatively motivated. That is, we are being motivated not so much to gain as to avoid loss. To that degree it is possible, although not very helpful, to say that when we behave badly we are seeking security. What is more useful, however, is to analyse from the behaviour the specific source of security which the individual seeks. If we can accurately define that longed-for security blanket and provide it without loss of our own integrity, we can at worst remove the cause of the unacceptable behaviour. In the ideal we can free the individual of fear and move them a small step toward self-actualisation.

The great advantage of Kaiser and Koffey's approach is that it enables us to:

- describe and recognise typical behaviours
- accurately assign motivators to the overt behaviours we see and experience
- develop specific and detailed strategies to satisfy the motive and remove the need for the negative behaviour
- change the behaviour to one which is constructive and acceptable
- use our skills to communicate effectively with someone whose behaviour is now acceptable and who is willing to give favourable attention to us and our ideas

CAN WE WIN THEM ALL?

Can the salesperson of manager 'win them all'? The short answer is 'yes'. The longer and more honest answer is 'yes – if and only if you have the essential knowledge, the skills which come from having that knowledge, and the time to exercise those skills.' There are still only 24 hours in the day. You *can* win them all, but in the real world you will probably choose to win only those which are worth winning.

This chapter provides the skills and knowledge. How and when you apply these remains your decision.

Looking back to Figure 8.1, there are some general behaviours which are typical of each segment:

- Those in the top left segment tend towards **aggressiveness** and **unpleasantness**.
- Those in the bottom left tend to demonstrate mistrust and avoidance of commitment.
- Those in the bottom right tend towards a level of agreeableness which can mask a deep insecurity and a total inability to fulfil commitments.
- Those at the top right show assertiveness and sometimes a somewhat authoritarian pursuit of quality, but they are also open to new ideas, actively seeking them as a means of improving both processes and results.

The characteristics of the person described by the top right-hand segment come closest to those of the self-actualising individual and are those which offer the best chance of a sale of an idea, product or service. The ideal is tough minded, but open minded – convince such an individual that what you have to offer makes sense in the face of their need and you have more than a customer, you have, as I have said before, an advocate.

The sections which follow take two typical but essentially different behaviour patterns from each segment, identify the strongest motivators for each, and provide specific step-by-step tactics to manage and change the behaviour, creating favourable attention to you and your ideas.

In each descriptive heading the first word used is the

controlling or major trait. So someone categorised as 'hostile–dominant' is drawn from the top left segment and is more *hostile* (appearing more to the left than any other part of the segment), while 'dominant–hostile' comes from the same general cluster, but for this individual *dominance* is the more important trait. If you do not frustrate this person's desire to be dominant they may not experience any need to be hostile, whereas the first kind of person get their kicks from aggression and allowing them to assume dominance tends to encourage ever greater aggression. This is because hostility is not the key motive, it is a behaviour aimed at providing the security which is craved.

The approach will be to describe:

- the key motivation
- the preferred strategy for satisfying the other person's need
- typical behaviours relevant to the strategy
- tactics for handling the behaviour and moving the other person toward eventual self-actualisation

HOSTILE–DOMINANT

MOTIVATION

Key motivation: desire for security
Motivation satisfaction strategy: attack is the best form of defence

TYPICAL BEHAVIOURS

Hostile–dominant people:

- Brag incessantly.
- Drop impressive names and relies on quoting and misquoting 'authorities' to win arguments.
- Interrupt impatiently and often.
- Show impatience quickly – finger drumming etc.
- Are unreasonably stubborn.
- Are argumentative without cause.
- Make broad generalisations and sweeping statements in argument.
- Are dogmatic and opinionated and ignore or attack contrary facts.

- Claim that 'everybody knows' whatever is uncertain or unlikely.
- Make frequent mutually inconsistent statements.
- React negatively without hearing the whole story.
- Make sarcastic comments.
- Try to belittle the product, the service, the idea, the salesperson and the company.
- Frequently personally abusive.
- Look for any opportunity to start a fight or take offence.
- Claim to have all the answers and never admit to mistakes.
- When things go wrong always look for others to blame.
- Must win the argument and will lie, invent or exaggerate to do so.

More than anything else this kind of person seeks to remain in charge of situations and people as a defensive mechanism. They cannot afford ever to admit to the possibility that a view other than their own has merit. They will bully, lie and insult to try to throw you off track. If they can get you to lose control, either by losing your temper or by driving you to despair, they will see that as a victory – and they need victories as they need victims.

Having created victims and thus being able to reject them and their ideas together, the surprisingly low self-esteem of the hostile–dominant person is bolstered and they feel a little more important and a little more secure.

You cannot afford to allow them the victory they crave, so you need to *keep your cool* whatever they throw at you and:

MANAGEMENT STRATEGIES

- Be courteous, but firm and assertive.
- Remember that you have nothing to lose. This person cannot operate in a vacuum. They must buy from someone, cooperate with someone and sometimes even follow someone else's advice or leadership.
- Ask closed questions frequently to establish and keep control.
- Avoid justifying yourself, your product or idea.
- Stick to demonstrable fact whenever possible.

- Test every gross assertion, broad generalisation or wild exaggeration politely but firmly.
- 'Are you really saying that *all*...?' should be the question which is constantly on your lips. If that is answered with a further exaggeration, continue to challenge it: 'Are you really saying that there are *no* exceptions?'
- Expect to meet both resistance to closing and exaggerated objections.

This is one situation where you simply *cannot* afford the other person to satisfy their needs – you must meet apparent strength with real strength. Use your communication skills to demonstrate that you cannot be bullied. If you can win this person's grudging respect your victory is their victory, as their new behaviour, at least with you, will be reinforced by success and may eventually become part of their dominant behavioural strategy.

DOMINANT–HOSTILE

MOTIVATION

Key motivation: need for status and autonomy
Motivation satisfaction strategy: precision and outward indicators of power

TYPICAL BEHAVIOURS

Dominant–hostile people:

- Are cold and detached.
- If angered remain cool but biting.
- Are angered if they believe their status is being underestimated or ignored.
- Are stubborn in their precise demand for proper attention in keeping with their importance.
- Make very precise statements, particularly when making a complaint.
- Are easily offended.
- Hold tenaciously to their evaluation of their own worth.
- React negatively to what they perceive as a personal slight or failure to take their complaint seriously.

- Avoid sarcasm, choosing instead to be cutting with accurate complaints which others might consider trivial.
- Avoid argument by telling you accurately and in detail where you are wrong.
- Demand efficiency and respect.
- Treat those whom they consider to be their inferiors with polite condescension.
- Treat their social superiors with self-confident courtesy.
- Respond badly to the opinions or experiences of others unless they see these others as their equals or of higher status.

Dominant–hostile people believe they should have high status. They consider recognition of that status as a right and insist on their rights at all times. In general, the more that you can build a relationship of mutual respect with this kind of person, the more likely it is that you will influence them. It is not appropriate to demean yourself. They only respect those they perceive as being of similar standing. If you hope to sell to this person your marketing effort should have been aimed at raising your personal reputation and status. Your demeanour during a face-to-face interview must be that of a high status equal engaged in mutual problem solving.

MANAGEMENT STRATEGIES

- Stress benefits which offer prestige, autonomy, recognition, control and freedom of action.
- Expect an early response of: 'I don't need you' and be prepared to live with temporary rejection until you prove yourself and your idea.
- Show conviction and strength, but avoid being, or appearing to be, cocky, aggressive, argumentative or overconfident.
- Be courteous always. Remember that courtesy is not mere politeness, but implies a genuine respect for others.
- Precede all questions with a benefit. This type of person expects to ask questions, not answer them, and you must sell them on giving the information you need.
- Only ask for information which you really need.

- Never use leading questions with this kind of person. They reject what they see as attempts to railroad them into a decision.
- Never allow this type to lose face. If they are wrong try to avoid mentioning it, or make it clear how and why their information may be inaccurate without indicating fault on their part.
- Credit the other person with good ideas even if they are yours, but do it with sensitivity. Remember that it is the customer's business that you want rather than their admiration if it comes to a choice. If possible, of course, have both.

HOSTILE–SUBMISSIVE

MOTIVATION

Key motivation: security expressed through abnormal demands for protection.

Motivation satisfaction strategy: excessively detailed 'what if' concerns

TYPICAL BEHAVIOURS

Hostile–submissive people:

- Express doubt about any statement made.
- Think up and express the most unlikely scenarios in which things could go wrong.
- Demand totally unreasonable guarantees.
- Insist on discussing hypothetical and very unlikely potential problems.
- Niggle and complain.
- Doubt the validity of any new idea.
- Incessantly ask questions, many of which are clearly impossible to answer.
- Give little, if any, information in return.
- If asked even the most innocuous of questions are likely to demand 'Why you want to know?'
- Are aggressive in physical demeanour and body language, but may be weak in behaviour.

- Avoid committing themselves to any agreement.
- Are generally pessimistic.
- Frequently assert that they have been badly treated by the many who have betrayed their trust in the past, but avoid giving any examples.
- Try to treat salespeople as untrustworthy inferiors.
- Accuse others of lying, not explicitly but by implication.

Hostile–submissive people tend to treat the whole world with excessive mistrust and, being more inclined toward hostility than defensiveness, know their 'rights' and seek to have them through unreasonable and unrealistic guarantees and warranted outcomes. They treat the whole world this way and there is nothing personal in any hostility shown. If their basic insecurity can be mitigated their behaviour will become more reasonable and more acceptable. It is important in trying to manage this behaviour that personal conflict is not allowed to develop, but the professional is always assertive and clearly in charge. Beware of being trapped into making promises which cannot be fulfilled. All that is promised must be delivered, or this kind of individual has more reason for their behaviour in the future. A great advantage of using the structured approach described in Chapters 6 and 7 is that it forces the individual rigorously to test the quality of their own ideas.

MANAGEMENT STRATEGIES

- Remain consistently patient in the face of repeated disbelief.
- Assure and reassure and use convincing examples to illustrate the safe application of your ideas.
- Give guarantees in writing where possible and avoid ambiguities or small print – if you cannot give an absolute guarantee, it is better to say so than to build the other person's mistrust through promises which cannot be honoured. You should always be seeking the long-term relationship – if someone like this believes that they can trust you they are unlikely to risk going to someone else.
- Stress benefits which provide stability, low risk, assured outcomes, proven value, permanence and durability.

- Show genuine concern for the customer's needs.
- Spend time exploring the buyer's key objective and don't expect them to tell you without a lot of arduous digging for information.
- Ask safe closed questions until they begin to open up, ask more open questions only when you are sure that they are at ease with you.
- Quote prestige users of your products, services or ideas. Prestige users offer a degree of security in the same way that a carefully developed brand image does.
- Be prepared to give this type of person a great deal of your time.
- Be sure that the investment of so much time is justified by the potential outcome. Once you start with this person you are committed to win, or be added to the long list of those who 'let them down', and if he criticises you there will always be some people to believe it and pass it on.

SUBMISSIVE–HOSTILE

MOTIVATION

Key motivation: fear of becoming committed or involved
Motivation satisfaction strategy: avoidance, withdrawal

When training motor dealer personnel they always recognise this type of behaviour. Few showroom salespeople have not experienced the dance around the showroom floor which takes place as they try to get close enough to 'meet and greet' this type of customer. Typical behaviour is to take a long, speculative look through the showroom window to ensure that no salesperson is visible close to the door. Entry is followed by a scuttle to whatever vehicle is furthest from the sales desks. If a salesperson approaches the customer moves away, maintaining the distance and making for the door if they can.

Submissive–hostile people:

- Maintain maximum possible physical distance from others
- Will actually seek to move away from salespeople or those perceived to be in authority
- Volunteer no information and tend to become extremely tight-lipped if questioned
- Say nothing unless sensitively probed
- When they do speak say as little as possible
- Prefer grunts and mumbles to audible expression of views and feelings: if forced to say something pick words with care
- Avoid commitment by any possible means including physical withdrawal when other avoidance strategies are unavailable
- Even feign illness to avoid involvement
- Are reluctant to take even minimal risk
- Appear tense and ill at ease when in company
- Refuse new ideas without listening to arguments if they can
- Are more inclined to accept well tried and safe products and ideas: if forced to a choice will invariably choose the low risk option
- Preferred behaviour is avoidance and procrastination, but if forced to a decision they will opt for 'no'
- Cling to habits, routine, rules and procedures
- Use rules and procedures, precedence or policy to avoid decision or justify rejection
- Take no personal responsibility for their own actions, blaming problems on others or things
- Shy away from any discussion of a 'personal' nature

This personality type's need for security extends even to their perceiving those who seek to help as threats.

Always try to avoid pressure, with one exception: if you have reached the stage where closing is appropriate, be totally assertive and supportive. Reassure until this person is confident that this time it will be all right. Identify where possible achievements from this person's past which were successful and apparently painless, and compare the new strategy detail by detail with the old.

- Approach slowly without unnecessary bonhomie or unbridled enthusiasm.
- Predetermine an acceptable reason for approach if this person shies away.
- Offer specific help where appropriate as an opportunity to get into conversation without perceived threat.
- Ask safe closed questions at first to initiate conversation. Safe questions are those to which this person can mumble a monosyllabic reply which is either noncommittal or socially so acceptable as to offer no threat.
- Keep well away from personal questions until the personal relationship is well established.
- Stress benefits which minimise or obviate risk.
- Link benefits logically to features so that there is no room for doubt that benefits will be enjoyed quickly and without risk.
- Present ideas slowly, a little information at a time, and ensure that each is fully accepted before moving on to the next.
- Avoid any sense of pressure through verbal or body language.
- Be unusually patient.
- Expect long periods of silence. Wait for responses regardless of how long it takes.
- Reward with body language and encouraging words any signs of opening up from this person.
- Exhibit genuine concern for their fears.
- Build trust slowly. When they are prepared to talk, listen carefully and demonstrate empathy at every opportunity.
- Guide firmly, but very gently.
- Accept all fears as real to them and understandable to you.
- Never joke about anything which they appear to take seriously.
- Bolster the individual's self-respect and self-image.
- If you choose to use leading questions at any point, be sure that they are non-threatening.

SUBMISSIVE–WARM

Key motivation: Above all things and regardless of the realities of the situation, this person wants to be loved. Affiliation at the extreme, desire to be liked gone mad.

Motivation satisfaction strategy: Tries to be all things to all people at all times.

Submissive–warm people:

- Become immediately and often falsely enthusiastic about any idea or product.
- Ramble incessantly. Frequently talk at length and with enthusiasm of unrelated subjects.
- Respond quickly and positively to any and all suggestions.
- Are eager to please and cause confusion by claiming any role or level of authority which is attributed to them, however false.
- Avoid raising objections and deny them even where they patently exist.
- Are readily convinced, but closing the sale is time consuming because of irrelevant gossip and red herrings.
- Seem to have all the time in the world for anything other than getting on with the job in hand, but if you suggest moving things forward they adopt a busy, busy approach to please you.
- Promise anything asked of them and rarely keep promises.
- After a long discussion in which they have given assurance that they are the decision maker, they change at the point of closing the sale to: 'Well I will put it to my boss. He has to make the final decision, but he always takes my advice.'
- If you ask to meet the boss you are fobbed you off with: 'He never sees (salespeople, other departmental managers etc.) He leaves this entirely to me...'
- If they sign an order they cancel through a third party, or you find your invoice is rejected because they lacked budget or authority and didn't like to say.
- Are often totally scathing of your competition ... and equally scathing about you to them.

MANAGEMENT STRATEGIES

People like this are the biggest time-wasters in business. They make conflicting promises to everyone and are able in the end to keep only those which are made to those with the greatest organisational power in their own company. What is worse, when they are 'found out' they become vindictive and, having become adept at doing harm to others in secret, they can be dangerous. They are weak, but what they lack in strength they more than make up in cunning and are ace survivors in a bureaucratic environment.

For prime examples of this type you probably need to think no further than your government – wherever you are. To manage this type of behaviour:

- Use closed questions to restrain garrulousness and excessive feigned enthusiasm.
- Be outgoing and friendly, but don't be sucked into irrelevances which cause you to lose control of the discussion.
- Stress benefits which provide personal acceptance, popularity and a chance to be seen as doing something for others.
- Focus on business, but give the other person some, limited, room to gossip.
- Personalise the discussion. They will ask you to use their first name on very short acquaintance. Do so – often.
- Guide their behaviour very firmly, but make your firmness feel like support. 'To please the people in your office start today...'
- Try to create a feeling that the pair of you are operating as a team.
- Probe for hidden objections and avoid being taken in by easy promises.
- If you get their signature on the order, follow up to ensure that they complete the transaction.

WARM–SUBMISSIVE

Key motivation: genuine sense of affiliation. A desire to do the maximum possible good for the maximum possible number. *Motivation satisfaction strategy*: seeks ways of actively pursuing the welfare of others.

MOTIVATION

Unlike submissive–warm people, warm–submissive people are probably very nice, kind and nurturing with a real concern for others. If they let that concern dominate behaviour they become almost as difficult to move to taking action as the earlier type. The difference in motivation makes little difference to the outcome. Whether you are primarily motivated by a desire to be liked at all costs in order to mitigate your own sense of insecurity, or you are immobilised by your genuine concern for others into taking no action which might conceivably damage anyone, there is a problem. Since the submissive–warm personality type are in a way trying to present themselves as concerned and caring, the differences in behaviour are subtle and often difficult to differentiate.

TYPICAL BEHAVIOURS

Warm–submissive people:

- Are intent on being pleasant.
- Respond supportively to most suggestions which do not threaten the well-being of others.
- Respond more negatively to suggestions which might damage others, but try to avoid conflict unless values and concern for others are seriously threatened, in which case they can become highly emotional. This can differentiate clearly from the behaviour of the submissive–warm who would say 'to hell with them' if they thought this is what you want to hear.
- Try to pick out the benefits of neutral ideas.
- Will procrastinate rather than reject ideas which are repugnant, but will not implement anything which harms others.
- Often give the impression that agreement has been reached when in fact strong reservations exist.

- Avoid raising objections unless the well-being of others is clearly threatened.
- Sometimes take on more than they can fulfil.
- Sometimes neglect important but impersonal work assignments in favour of helping someone out.
- Are at the forefront of socially valuable activities, charity collections, etc.

MANAGEMENT STRATEGIES

If this type of individual can be presented with ideas which genuinely offer the maximum good to the maximum number, they will implement them with enthusiasm. The difficulty comes when hard decisions must be made. Unlike the submissive–warm who only want to be liked as a defence to their own sense of insecurity, the warm–submissive genuinely seek to do good for others and will fight for what they believe is right if they must. A simple example: assume that headcount restrictions have been imposed at a level which creates a number of compulsory redundancies. The submissive–warm will pick out those who have threatened or rejected them and try to pervert whatever system is in place to lose these 'ungrateful' people their jobs. The warm–submissive will, in contrast, try to find ways by which the loss of jobs can be avoided altogether – or delayed for as long as possible. (See also Chapter 5.)

- Try to present ideas so that the benefits to people rather than institutions are emphasised.
- Where this is impossible do not assume that a lack of overt opposition means agreement or commitment.
- Try to create a role which maximises opportunities for personal interaction.
- Monitor and supervise implementation not only of tough decisions but also of anything which is impersonal and important.

WARM–DOMINANT AND DOMINANT–WARM

This quartile and the people it represents were seen as the ideal by Lefton and Buzotta in their analysis of the work of Kaiser and Koffey. The purpose of the tactics described under each of the problem behavioural types is to move their behaviour from the difficult toward this perceived archetype of preferred leadership conduct. Human nature is never quite that simple. Just as it is easier in general to demotivate than it is to motivate others, so it is perfectly possible to inadvertently move people from this open and accessible mode of behaviour toward or into one of the more difficult segments. That is another reason it is essential for managers and salespeople to learn and practise techniques which are known to build rapport and long-term individual relationships, rather than indulge in short-term approaches which get an immediate response, but build a barrier of defensiveness for the future.

POSITIVE BEHAVIOURAL TRAITS

Warm–dominant and dominant–warm people:

- Express views clearly and frankly.
- Cut short anything which they perceive as 'bull'.
- Reject political solutions and question the motives of those who suggest a politically acceptable approach.
- Ask pertinent and searching questions.
- Probe tirelessly for the fullest answer.
- Admit their own lack of understanding or lack of knowledge.
- Concentrate attention on what can be achieved.
- Place high demands on others' values and principles as well as their own.
- Demand high levels of achievement but keep their demands within the confines of the individual's (stretched) abilities.
- Act naturally and appear comfortable with their role.
- Comment frequently on the beauty of nature when appropriate and seem to see, in the commonplace, unusual worth with a little more clarity than most.
- Express themselves in simple straightforward words.
- Make no attempt to impress others.

- Avoid blaming others.
- Seek out problems for the joy of finding novel and attractive solutions.
- Are comfortable to own a problem.
- Are clear about their goals and objectives.
- Hold strong views on what is right and acceptable and reject any idea that what is ethically wrong can be defended because it is 'practical'.
- Are comfortable when solitary or in company and show no concern about either condition.
- In times of worry still manage to sleep well, have an undisturbed appetite and treat their situation with genuine humour.
- Are loyal to the group, but express loyalty in terms of challenge to the group to reach ever higher standards.
- Avoid change for its own sake.
- Actively seek opportunities for self-development.
- Are open to new ideas even when the established way still appears to work.
- Challenge ideas to ensure that they are ecologically sound: that is, they harm no one and nothing.
- Express and live up to a passionate belief in the potential goodwill of people.
- Show an exceptional degree of understanding for the feelings of others.
- Treat feelings as facts in any situation.
- Use delegation to encourage the personal and professional growth of others.
- Select for close colleagues an elite based on character, capacity and talent.
- Seek long-term relationships rather than easy acquaintance and may seem somewhat distant until respect and liking are earned.
- Are truly courteous rather than merely polite in that they show respect for the integrity and values of others.
- Have a gentle sense of humour and any jokes are likely to be generalised or focused only on themselves.
- Are creative and build easily on ideas, without taking over the ideas of others.

No one is without fault. Less desirable traits of warm–dominant and dominant–warm people may include:

- Prolonged searching for the ideal solution when the acceptable is at hand.
- A tendency to delegate rapidly, followed by taking over 'to show how it is done'.
- They will change your best ideas to improve them – but at least they will acknowledge the idea as yours.

You are assured of a careful, although possibly challenging hearing from this type of person. They will decide very much on the basis of fact and their own opportunity to build in added value. Provide them with the full facts as concisely as possible, with emphasis on how your idea can solve their problem or improve their process. The structured approach outlined in Chapter 4 is ideal because it enables a comprehensive and logical case to be put concisely.

MANAGEMENT STRATEGIES

SUMMARY

In influence strategy you can, if you wish, win them all – but just as you must decide for yourself what is and what is not an ethical use of influence technology, you also need to consider the time expended against the value of the outcome.

Behaviour is the product of previous experience and present motivation. Different strategies for achieving security can lead to different behaviours, any of which can make any of us a pain in the neck. The reduction of fear can do much to enable us to grow in maturity toward the ultimate of self-actualisation. Humans are far from perfect, but sometimes your actions as an influence professional can help someone to take a step on the road towards perfection.

9 Women on Top

> **WHAT YOU WILL GAIN FROM THIS CHAPTER**
>
> - An understanding of why, in today's world, the influencing style which is more effective is that which tends to be practised by women.
> - The knowledge that such a style is a product of culture, not of nature.
> - A game plan for ensuring the best of both genders is present in your own approach.

Women are so much nicer than people.

(Quentin Crisp)

Both men and women are trapped in the prisons of gender...but the situation is is far from symmetrical; men are the oppressors and women the oppressed.

(M. Taylor)

Peter Medawar, top scientist, Nobel laureate and arguably the best writer on science in the twentieth century, argued that the failure of western culture to put more women at the head of organisations of every kind, business, scientific or government, deprived us of full use of half the world's talent. I am somewhat reticent to contradict such a great man, but I must. Sir Peter was wrong. Failure to enable and encourage women to fully exploit their talents has deprived us of a great deal more than half of our skill and knowledge store. Women have more to contribute than mere equality of the sexes might denote.

At conferences and elsewhere when I mention in passing the natural superiority of women as consultants, executives and salespeople, the response tends to be one of irritated incredulity from the men and pleased disbelief from the women. Since the men are almost always in the majority, it is not a view that necessarily makes me popular. I believe that we have much to gain from its explanation, so I think that it is time I placed all my cards firmly on the table.

Women are potentially superior consultants, executives and salespeople for two major reasons, one psychological and one cultural.

Let me explore the cultural first. In most, if not all, so-called advanced societies, the genders have different approaches to communication. Men are said to communicate asymmetrically, while women's approaches are symmetrical. What, then, are the crucial differences and how do these differences create an uneven standard of performance which tilts the quality advantage toward the female?

THE CULTURAL
REASON

Asymmetrical communication is defined as that which is aimed at emphasising the differences between people. To put it baldly, men tend to use communication to identify, challenge, assert or reinforce perceived differences of status.

Imagine a couple in an expensive restaurant. The service has been slow and surly, the food poorly cooked, the wine served at the incorrect temperature, and cutlery or glasses have shown that unpleasant smearing which only comes from the use of unchecked machine washing. The manager comes over to ask if everything is satisfactory. In keeping with the standards of the restaurant, his concern is belied by the fact that he starts to move away from the table without waiting for a reply. As far as the male customer is concerned this is the last of a number of particularly rank straws. Icy and cutting or loud and dominant according to taste, he starts to tell the manager in clear and unambiguous terms precisely what he thinks of him, his restaurant, food and staff. At first the manager attempts to shrug off the criticism or treat it as a piece of good-humoured joshing, an example of western male bonding. Then he tries to defend himself and his establishment. But the customer continues his unanswerable litany of complaint. At last — or very soon, according to the quality of the onslaught — the manager is reduced to a gibbering wreck. The customer, with a final grand gesture, tears up the bill and with the admonition not to expect his return to that restaurant until some time after hell freezes over, escorts his embarrassed partner to the door.

Hungry and ill tempered, his conversation on the journey home fluctuates between new outbursts of anger over the way that the evening has been ruined, and triumphant remembrances of the specific barbs with which he defeated the restaurant manager. If his partner fails to recognise his achievements with sufficient deference and admiration, his ill-temper is turned on her.

Contrast this only mildly exaggerated account with what might happen were two women diners to share the same lousy service. The first difference is that women generally draw the waiter's attention to the first problem as soon as they recognise it. Rather than the very public cleaning of cutlery and glass with a napkin that men tend to indulge in, they would ask the waiter to replace the offending articles, inferring at the same time how they understand that pressures of time can cause problems in the kitchen and elsewhere. If the food is badly cooked or not to their taste they would ask the waiter to return it to the kitchen and replace it with a preferred alternative. At every stage they will be trying to turn the waiter from surly antagonist to helpful friend.

When the manager comes to the table to exercise his perfunctory 'any complaints' ritual, they calmly indicate that things have not been perfect, but that, through the good offices of their friend the waiter, problems have been ameliorated or overcome. They leave the restaurant relaxed and well fed and with the knowledge that, should they ever decide to return, food and service will be noticeably better and they will be treated as very special customers.

I admitted to a degree of exaggeration, but the above is probably exaggerated only in the range of complaints, not in the reaction to them. But potential domination is not the only card which men seek to play. Where men see themselves as having a decent fighting chance, and I choose my words with care, of coming out on top, they tend to attempt to take and maintain control. Where it is clear that the other will win any battle, men tend to accept and even reinforce their subservience. If the worst comes to the worst, there is a touch of Uriah Heep in most of us, although it usually takes a great deal to bring it out.

Women, on the contrary, tend to ignore status differences and build instead a relationship in which status is an irrelevance. There are, of course major exceptions. In the atavistic world of politics it has become almost a requirement of women that if they want to hold high office they must have more and bigger balls than the men around them. When I was a boy a favoured insult in the pit villages that my family came from was 'You'll never be half the man your mother was.' The expectations which mould the behaviour of senior politicians make this a truism when you consider national leaders as different in policy, but similar in public perception, as Lady Thatcher, Golda Meir, Sirima Bandaranaike or Benazir Bhutto.

One of the most powerful anti-feminist books of recent years is *Male Bonding* by the illustrious biologist Lionel Tiger. In this tightly argued book Tiger puts a strong case that men have the edge in building relationships as exemplified by male bonding. A strong case, but it has one crucial weakness. Male bonding is an asymmetrical relationship: one in which status is not merely reflected, it is critical.

There has always been the captain and the star of the team, the hero of the hunt and even the brain of the dorm. Whatever attribute is selected by the environment to be the source of status, it provides the framework around which bonding occurs. If you have it you're in. If you don't you may still get in, but only on your knees as licensed buffoon or sychophant.

The environment in which we now operate demands something more subtle than male bonding based on selected skills and adulation. In a period of rapid change, all information may be valuable regardless of whether it comes from a high status individual. Increasingly we are in a world where consensus is the only hope of having sufficient information on which to base decisions. We need to create relationships in which information flows freely and confidently even from those who fail to understand its import. This will not happen with an insider crowd or elite. Everyone needs to be or become a knowledge worker.

What about male bonding?

It is not only a matter of data. Commitment is essential, and for commitment we cannot ignore motives, emotions, feelings and perceptions. Feelings are and have always been part of the key facts. Traditional male bonding creates insiders and outsiders and you cannot expect commitment or input from outsiders.

Finally, male bonding creates a particular mindset. A fixed mindset is the enemy of creativity and we need creativity today more than ever before. Symmetrical relationships sensitive to unspoken feelings are essential.

Marketing profession = marketing status

Successful consultants and other professionals, including surgeons and barristers, market their services using proven tactics which enhance their reputation and status in the eyes of their potential clients. (For details of how see my *High Income Consulting*.) In our society, although things are changing, both client and consultant are usually male. This prefabrication of reputation means that first critical face-to-face meeting does not deteriorate in a barren contest for status. To have your client or patient hold you just a little bit in awe has been the key strategy to ensure easy acquiesence, fat contracts and fatter fees.

Women's communication style in our culture is, as I have said, symmetrical. It is aimed at reinforcing the similarities between people. More, it is aimed specifically at building warm relationships. Such communication will not invariably attract the biggest fees or the highest prices, but the ability to get close to others, fully share their hopes and dreams and respond honestly but with empathy does provide the best chance of high quality interactions. And people choose to repeat high quality interactions.

Part of the way in which the world, particularly the business world, is changing is in the emergence of a desire that is almost strong enough to be considered a goal of building and sustaining long-term relationships. Thus major corporations increasingly share intelligence, experience and skills with 'strategic allies'.

Nature or nurture?

The differences of style and content of male and female communication are entirely the result of nurture, they have little to do with nature. No one can have any doubt that a woman can assume the self-promoting, status-building role in our society with great personal success. If she were limited to the tendencies of her gender it is unlikely that the hard edge could be maintained. If a woman can adopt male behaviour patterns when it suits her, it is likely that a man can use some of the best of woman's tactics, if it helps to achieve a worthwhile goal, without loss of self-esteem. Earlier chapters developed tactics which are equally valid for male and female and which are extremely effective in building and keeping relationships.

A second example of the cultural basis of gender differences is rather more fun to contemplate. Anthropologists draw attention to the Vakinankaratra of Madagascar. In this small society the primary motivation of male communication is to build relationships and avoid confrontation. So ingrained is this motive that if a male is angered by some behaviour of another he is incapable of expressing his negative feelings. He incites a female relative or friend to speak the necessary harsh words for him while he stands by expressing delicate sentiments aimed at almost immediate rebuilding of interpersonal bridges. Men of the Vakinankaratra are culturally incapable of verbally attacking another, expressing assertiveness, haggling in the marketplace, reprimanding children or even offering the expression of mild generalised disapproval.

I stress the cultural nature of these sexual archetypes because culture, by definition, is learned behaviour, which means that a new type of androgyny is possible. Men can continue to use status building as the key to their marketing effort while learning symmetrical approaches for face-to-face communication. This oils the wheels without damaging professional standing or earning capacity. Indeed, it has the opposite effect. We have all had the experience of meeting a high status individual who turns out to be totally charming 'in the flesh'. We seldom think less of such people for being a pleasure to meet.

At the same time, women can confidently enhance the use of what they will have come to believe is their 'natural' conversational style while learning how to market their skills with personal and professional status-building techniques.

Everyone, regardless of gender should be comfortable, consistent and happy: most of all, the client who can buy the services of a high status expert with total confidence and enjoy the experience. A special kind of added value comes from developing a long-term relationship with a reliable source of professional support.

THE PSYCHOLOGICAL REASON

Psychology is a slightly different situation. Our cognitive processes and our behaviour are partly learned, partly genetically determined. How much is, or can be, learned and how much is genetic is open to discussion, and psychologists argue about it *post nauseam*. The fact remains that much learning is possible, even in situations where genes appear to rule. That being so, men have reason to consider and seek to emulate the natural psychological superiority of women.

To attempt to create a gender personality profile would do violence to the obvious fact that, man or woman, all humankind is infinitely variable. What we do have, however, as the result of a number of research programmes, is a personality profile which is true of the superior consultant. I suggest, tentatively, that these traits, taken as a broad generalisation, tend to be more frequently true of women than they are of men.

The primary trait is that of having a sense of vocation driven by the desire to do the maximum good for others: a valuing of the significance of what is being done allied to a desire to be nurturing. This is in direct contrast to the more 'masculine' trait of seeing all business situations as an actual or potential competition in which the primary aim is to win. To put it another way, the successful consultant, male or female, has a greater leaning toward symmetrical communication. The less effective will use power or sleight of hand to win, with all too often less than ideal outcomes for the client: the ultimate in asymmetry.

A good consultant is committed to the development of others, whether those others be individuals or organisations. In pursuing this goal the individual consultant often must be self-effacing and underplay their own importance in the situation. Personal and organisational growth in any new situation is often dependent on the timely and sensitive support and coaching of those who must make it happen by those who know how: another example of extended and focused symmetrical behaviour. Affiliation, the building of relationships with others, is an obvious result of symmetry. It is also a crucial behavioural trait of consultants.

The ability to focus on the relevant detail, to draw the essentials from complexity, is by no means unique to women, but generations of intelligence testing suggest that woman's demonstrated superiority in linguistic and mathematical thinking may rest heavily on their superior ability to identify and concentrate on the important rather than being, as men often are, seduced by the whole, by the spatial imperative. This is not to argue that men are weak in analytic thinking. Most of us, however, can lay little claim to greatness, and while males dominate the extremes of intellect, producing geniuses and cretins in far greater numbers than do women, in the middle regions where most of our capacities lie, women tend to perform better on the more analytic tasks.

That then, within the constraints of a short chapter, is the foundation for my claim that women have a greater given potential to achieve in the profession of consultancy than do their male colleagues and competitors. And leader, salesperson or parent, we must become credible *consultants* to succeed in a volatile world.

A NEW ANDROGYNY

Female superiority is an accident of culture allied to a certain limited predisposition. It is real, but it is by no means beyond the grasp of men. By using the best of both styles flexibly and sensitively, both sexes can offer superior service to their customers, staff and colleagues while increasing their own income opportunities and creating the relationships which lead to more effectiveness and more repeat and referral business. In short, women have the edge, but it doesn't have to stay that way; a new androgyny could be to the benefit of all.

Room at the top is limited. Many may aspire to the dominant position, but by the laws of simple arithmetic few can attain it. If more women can be among that few it is possible, through building closer, more lasting and warmer relationships, that they could create a fairer, saner, less competitive world. Until now it has been difficult if not impossible for women to reach the pinnacle without adopting the competitiveness which characterises male behaviour. For business leadership a recent quote from Ann Gloag in the *Sunday Express* says it all.

A woman in business has to look like a lady, act like a man and work like a dog.

BUSINESS IN THE LEAD

There is hope, however. Through proactive strategic thinking an as yet small but growing core of business leaders is seeking to recreate business in a form which enables the thinker to dominate. Recognition of the realities of the changing world will focus the desire to dominate in the markets, but the tools of dominance will be the feminine ones of relationship building and maintenance. In such a world women in business will be able to succeed and retain their integrity as representatives of their gender.

For many years psychologists inadvertently pandered to gender stereotypes by developing psychometric tests in which male and female gender descriptions were seen as mutually exclusive. With her Sex Role Inventory (1974) Sandra Bem heralded the dawn of androgyny. Bem collected a total of 400 gender-based descriptions which she carefully filtered down to 40 which were testable – 20 for each gender. To this she added a further 20 which were gender neutral, but which were carefully selected to enable the administering psychologist to recognise any attempt on the part of the subject to gloss the test with socially acceptable answers.

Unlike her predecessors, however, she designed her test so that each trait was measured without reference to an alternative. At last the psychology profession belatedly began to put aside the idea that males were in all circumstances aggressively masculine and that women were beguilingly vampish or ultra-innocent on every occasion. Psychology caught up with popular literature and began to accept that men could be strong and tender or gentle and tough – and so could women.

Bem successfully separated the concepts of gender stereotype and emotional well-being for the first time. By disentangling the unrelated concepts of sex typing and mental health she enabled us to begin to focus on the societal consequences of sex-role-bound behaviour.

BEM SEX ROLE INVENTORY – TRAITS AND BEHAVIOURS

Male	Female	Neutral
Acts as leader	Affectionate	Adaptable
Aggressive	Cheerful	Concerted
Ambitious	Childlike	Conscientious
Analytical	Compassionate	Conventional
Assertive	Does not use	Friendly
Athletic	harsh language	Happy
Competitive	Eager to soothe	Helpful
Defends own	hurt feelings	Inefficient
beliefs	Feminine	Jealous
Dominant	Flatterable	Likeable
Forceful	Gentle	Moody
Has leadership	Gullible	Reliable
abilities	Loves children	Secretive
Independent	Loyal	Sincere
Individualistic	Sensitive to	Solemn
Makes decisions	needs of others	Tactful
easily	Shy	Theatrical
Masculine	Soft spoken	Truthful
Self reliant	Sympathetic	Unpredictable
Self sufficient	Tender	Unsystematic
Strong personality	Understanding	
Willing to take	Warm	
a stand	Yielding	
Willing to take		
risks		

Bem's hope was, and doubtless still is, that:

in a society where rigid sex role differentiation has already
outlived its usefulness, perhaps an androgynous person will
come to define a more human standard of psychological
health.

A move toward androgyny need not, and should not merge and
devalue masculine and feminine. Gender awareness is an early
and important part of self-awareness, which in turn is the
foundation of self-worth. The new androgyny is characterised by

sensitive situational analysis and the ability to moderate the competitive, aggressive elements of behaviour where such elements are counterproductive. Androgyny, like listening, is an 'in–out' affair. Sensitivity is a skill of which we are all capable regardless of gender.

SUMMARY

The needs of modern business and of tomorrow's society require a sensitive blend of masculine and feminine communication styles. Since masculine styles have dominated our culture for centuries, concentration needs now to be focused on the feminine.

We should strive, sensitively and in appropriate circumstances to escape from sex role stereotyping. The new androgyny should not be exaggerated: it should be situation specific.

Cross-gender skills should be consciously applied in pursuit of ethical goals.

Women should:

- Be confident in the relevance of their culturally evolved skills and abilities in a changing world.
- Avoid the temptation to believe that 'in what is still a man's world' macho behaviour is most effective.
- Do what they do best and most naturally without undue self-consciousness.

Men should:

- Recognise that the world, and people's expectations, are changing.
- Try to avoid the 'rutting stag' syndrome of locking antlers with all that they meet to establish who has the power in any situation.
- Use the skills of Chapters 3, 5 and (above all?) this chapter sensitively to build confidence and rapport in every encounter.

The Power Game 10

WHAT YOU WILL GAIN FROM THIS CHAPTER

● Leadership and influence demand the exercise of power
● An understanding of the sources of personal power
● How to assess your personal power potential
● How to use power effectively and ethically

A leader is best when people barely know he exists. When his work is done, his aim fulfilled, they will say: 'We did it all ourselves.'
(Lao Tsu)

Powerlessness corrupts and absolute powerlessness corrupts absolutely.
(Rosabeth Moss Kanter)

I'm not convinced that all power corrupts. After all this book is, in effect, a game plan for benevolent despots. Those who would or do manage the behaviour of others exercise power and if you exercise power I believe that you ought to do so with your mind uncluttered by clichés and your eyes wide open. (There's a cliché if ever I wrote one.)

POWER GAMES ARE ESSENTIAL GAMES

So let us look at power. There is personal power and there is organisational power – and just to make matters more confused there is personal power applied to reach organisational goals, and there is organisational power perverted to meet purely personal needs. Does all this matter?

David MacClelland completed some unique research into what made leaders tick. His conclusions were that leaders are motivated to different degrees by three basic needs:

- achievement
- affiliation

and

- power

and the greatest of these is power.

That sounds neat, but it is not exactly what either I or MacClelland meant. Power is not necessarily the greatest motivator of those who aspire to leadership. Many are more motivated by a drive to achieve. We care more about standards and quality than we do about people's feelings or the exercise of power. For us it is not enough to get things done. We need to get things done better. And we tend to be dismissive of those who fail to meet the high standards which we set for them. Do you see how the motivation to achieve is inimical to effective leadership? If you do you may take some pride in seeing a little more clearly than MacClelland did in his original research.

AN EXPERIMENT WITH LEADERS OF THE FUTURE

Imagine that you are a bright young student at an Ivy League university in the US. Your university has a cherished and honourable history of providing your country with its leaders in industry, commerce and politics. Great things are expected of you and your peers. Graduation will entitle you to a fast-track run straight to the top in business or politics. You are already one of the chosen. There is no reason why you should put a limit on your ambition. Today the ivy-covered walls – tomorrow the White House.

A young professor of psychology with an interest in leadership regards you as an ideal object of study. He has designed a series of experiments. For the sake of brevity I will describe only one.

A puzzle which has been tested on a sufficient range of people of your high educational level is said to be able to conclude that, even among the brightest, the chances of solving it are only one in three. The puzzle has been carefully designed not to require the application of specialist knowledge. It defeats two out of three of the best young brains for a very simple reason: it is very challenging.

You are made an offer. You can win a small but valuable reward by electing to be tested in one of two ways. You can attempt to solve the puzzle knowing that the chances are stacked two to one against you. Thus you will expend a good deal of effort and you will probably fail. The alternative offer presents you with an equal risk of failure and the same opportunity to win the same reward, but with no discernable effort or expenditure of time. You are offered one throw of an honest die and are challenged to throw either a two or a four. Again, a two to one against shot. The choice is yours: blood, sweat and tears (I speak only figuratively), or luck. Which would you choose?

If you chose the problem you are in good company. By far the majority of MacClelland's subjects chose to struggle with it too. MacClelland therefore reasoned like this: these people are the leaders of the future, they clearly demonstrate a preference for challenge over luck. Therefore leaders tend to be motivated by the need for personal achievement.

Other experiments showed that, although all were motivated somewhat by the need to have and apply power and to build and sustain relationships, never was the choice so clearly in favour of either power or affiliation as it was for achievement. So was MacClelland was right? Well, no – and he was, to his great credit, the first to see the holes in his experimental method.

First, the people on whom the experiment had been carried out were not leaders, but simply those who through a somewhat doubtful method of selection would probably become leaders in the future. Secondly, they were in an environment in which personal academic achievement was highly regarded. Even in university sport where team success is important, it is the individual contribution of the star which makes heroes – the less spectacular contribution of the ideal team player is virtually invisible. Thirdly, and perhaps most importantly, there is no quantified evidence that those who achieve positions of leadership through privilege, whether of birth or education, make *good* leaders. Few comparisons are made because too often such people are the only leaders we have.

I strongly recommend those who wish to read more deeply on this and many other aspects of leadership to consult Alistair Mant's brilliant book, *Leaders We Deserve*.

Ironically, and in part the reason I have dwelt on this particular experiment, a simple survey carried out among leaders in the UK, in which those who were deemed to have been the most successful were asked to identify the key skill which had led to their success, isolated a single 'skill' which it was claimed was the one essential attribute. Almost all of those surveyed attributed their success to this skill. It was the skill of *luck*. Perhaps those who chose to roll the die had the clearest view of what leads to success.

As I said, MacClelland was among the first to recognise the problem his research had raised and amended his key motivator on the back of that research to be power. Why power, why not achievement?

ACHIEVEMENT

Why am I so adamant that someone who is highly achievement motivated is likely to fail? Leaders need to understand that in the end it is impossible for them to do everything themselves. But what of someone who, in an attempt to meet their deep-seated motivational needs, sets unusually high standards of attainment for themselves and others? Can they really keep their nose out of even the the most menial of tasks and leave it to others? It is very unlikely. They fully understand that they must delegate. They are total believers in developing the skills and abilities of their team. Rationally there is no problem. But emotionally it is a different matter.

They delegate a task: they explain the desired outcome, detail the way it should be done, underline the importance of the task and step back. They watch in agony while the subordinate tries their best. The manager tries to be patient, but finally their self-control breaks. They elbow their erstwhile protégé to one side: 'Let me show you how it's done!'

Achievers, as MacClelland's later research and very succesful training programmes clarified, make good entrepreneurs, particularly if they operate as loners in a service industry.

What then of our third category, those whose primary motivation is affiliation? Are they successful as leaders?

There are people in this world who, as I have detailed in Chapter 8, are motivated above all things by a desire to be loved by everyone. The evidence is that their motivation and the unrealistic demands which it creates arise from a potent sense of insecurity. Imagine the leadership style of such a person.

Deeply insecure and constantly under emotional pressure to be popular, will this person be able to take the tough decision and see it through? Will they be able to take any decision at all which is not driven, at best, by a desire to avoid harm to anyone? This motivation effects a range of people from the genuinely caring to the near psychotic, whom I have described elsewhere. Good or bad, getting things done is not a hallmark of their character. And at the last, getting things done is what leadership is all about. Getting things done demands the exercise of power.

THE ANATOMY OF POWER

Kenneth Galbraith, the great economic thinker, wrote an excellent book on power in the political and economic world. He coined the word *condign* to describe most people's rather off-balance view of what we mean when we talk of power.

Condign power is where one person or organisation is in a position to force compliance. It is, to misquote Edward Heath, the *unacceptable face of power*, and many decent people feel so strongly about it that they consign all power to the dustbin of experience. Sadly, the avoidance of power is not an option. You either exercise power or you are subject to it. Or in the real world, sometimes you wield power and sometimes power is wielded over you. Leader or salesperson, you must be in control most of the time so, like it or not, you still need to understand the power you have if you are to use it wisely.

One can take some satisfaction from the fact that those who are motivated by affiliation can learn to use power, and when they do so their natural inclination may be to use it in the interests of others. Those whose primary motive is achievement will address the learning of the use of power as we address so many things. We will seek to do it well to start with and better thereafter.

Those who are already driven by the need to excercise power need to learn only that power must be used, for maximum success, as the means of getting things done in the organisational setting. Power is not a personal possession; it is not first prize in an ego competition.

AUTOGENIC PERSONAL AUTHORITY ANALYSIS

The word *autogenic* delights me. It can be crudely defined as meaning 'do it yourself', a wonderfully homely meaning for a grand sounding word. What follows is, if you like to see it that way, an autogenic test of your understanding of the power which you wield in the workplace or elsewhere.

Please consider which of the following statements is true of you:

Resource power

People do as I require because I control resources which they value

Yes ☐ No ☐

Information power

I can influence the behaviour of others because I have access to information which they need or desire

Yes ☐ No ☐

Position (or legitimate) power

I have power over others because I hold a powerful position in the social or business heirarchy. I bear an invisible label which says 'I'm in charge'

Yes ☐ No ☐

Proxy power

People do as I require because I have friends in high places

Yes ☐ No ☐

Reward power

People do as I want because I can reward those who comply with my wishes

Yes ☐   No ☐

Sanctions power

People do as I require because I can punish those who don't

Yes ☐   No ☐

Expert power

People do as I wish because they respect my knowledge and expertise

Yes ☐   No ☐

Personal (or referent) power

People do as I wish because they like me and want to model their behaviour on mine

Yes ☐   No ☐

Status power

People do as I wish because I have status in the group. I may be the oldest, the longest serving, the only one with a degree or whatever

Yes ☐   No ☐

Charisma power

People do as I wish because they are bowled over by my personality, vision, enthusiasm and/or charm

Yes ☐   No ☐

Favour power

People do as I wish because I build a bank balance of favours and call them in when I need compliance

Yes ☐   No ☐

Yes ☐   No ☐

Technical power

People do as I wish because I know how to influence behaviour and apply my knowledge with skill

Yes ☐   No ☐

Which of these sources of power do I use most frequently?

Which would I like to have more of?

Which am I least comfortable about using?

If I asked those who know me best at work or in the family would they agree with my analysis of the sources of my power?

Yes ☐   No ☐

If the answer to the question above is 'No', am I right or are they?

Me ☐   Them ☐

How might I access the source of power of which I want more?

Why all this interest in the sources of power? It has always been argued that although many fortunate and talented people have unconscious competence they, like the rest of us, are best able to optimise the application of their gifts if they develop conscious skills. You may have success through the unconscious application of a specific type of power. If you can do well unconsciously, the chances are that conscious skill development will turn success into triumph.

POWER IS THE KEY

Learn about power. Take a cold, clear look at what you have going for you and use it to get things done. If you don't like what you have, develop a power source with which you feel comfortable and use it, because, as with so many things in life, what you don't use you lose.

There is a form of power which we all have, which goes under the name of the *idiosyncracy balance.* It is a cousin of legitimate or positional power. It is ethereal – here today and possibly gone tomorrow, but while you have it it can give you a flying start.

CAN YOU BALANCE YOUR IDIOSYNCRACY?

Politicians taking a leadership role are always described in the popular press as enjoying 100 days in which they are virtually fire-proof. It seems that the voting public give those whom we have recently elected around three months during which we take the view that it's early days yet and unfair to ask for too much by way of results. Come day 101, however, and we expect to have something to show for our long-suffering forbearance. Of course politicians, being human, dislike the sudden upsurge of criticism. Being pragmatists, however, they console themselves with the thought that it's four years or more to the next election, by which time a judicious tax cut or two will be enough to change their standing, or lack of it, in the polls.

In business it's not quite so simple. We all get our equivalent of the 100 days. But at the end we have either sown the seeds of success and had the odd triumph or two, or we make way for the informal leader. We may keep the grand title, the company car and the fancy office, but as far as influence is concerned, we either perform or we are finished with the people who are most important to us – our team.

In simple language it works like this. Have you ever seen someone raised to a position of leadership within an organisation and thought something along the lines of:

> My God, where did they dig him up from? If ignorance is bliss
> this guy appears to be in the running for the title 'world's
> happiest man'. He looks a total idiot to me, but I guess he must
> have something going for him or they never would have given
> him the job. Perhaps I had better give him the benefit of the
> doubt and just see what happens.

That is idiosyncracy balance in action. You withhold judgement
for a while and either the new leader performs and you concede
that those above knew what they were doing after all, or he fails
and your first impression is reinforced. Success is the magic
ingredient which turns a group into a team. Teams only exist in
order that together they can achieve what they are unable to
achieve alone. They demand success of their leaders.

Research shows that groups who have a leader of courage and
integrity who goes to bat for them loyally whenever the need
emerges, but who always comes back with a bloody nose, hold
such a leader in far less esteem than they do a conniving
poltroon who only sticks their head up out of the trench when
victory is certain. No leader who fails to provide their team with
easy and early success is a hero to anyone, no matter how
audacious his failures. There comes a time when it is more
comfortable all round just to ignore the hierarchy and second a
member of the team to assume the leadership role informally.
They too must bring success or their leadership tenure is
equally short lived.

Leadership is like a bank account. And like most bank
accounts there is a strict limit to how long you can hope to be
overdrawn. With each success a leader's balance of credibility
grows, with each bloody nose it declines. If they do nothing in an
attempt to avoid risk, it slowly seeps away and they finally lose
out, although they may have a somewhat longer tenure than the
spectacular calamity on legs.

HOW DO YOU LEAD SELF-DIRECTED TEAMS?

Even the present fashion for empowerment or self-directed teams does not mean that the need for strong leadership is lessened, nor is the leader's dependence on results. With an empowered team the leader still has accountability not merely upwards but with the team themselves. That means that the leader must:

- retain a full understanding of what is happening within the team
- set a clear, unambiguous direction for the team, and ensure that people remain on course
- offer support, open doors and clear the way for action without taking over from those delegated to do the job
- make decisions which others cannot, either because of lack of time, information or knowledge
- continuously assess performance, reward progress and support individual and team development
- build trust through shared success and share information and knowledge whenever it is possible to do so

and most of all:

- select and apply their 'power tools' with judgement and diligence to ensure that the team enjoy the success that they crave

In the next chapter I defend the much maligned behaviourists because I believe that much of their work has enabled the development of models which add significantly to our understanding of behaviour – human and animal. There is, however, one type of experiment which sickens me and for which they are largely responsible. This is where an animal is subjected to pain and suffering and where the scientist, realising that the results cannot be simply extrapolated to human subjects, designs a far less traumatic experiment which makes the earlier torture of a harmless animal as unnecessary as it is meaningless.

HOW DO YOU KILL A RAT THROUGH INDUCED DEPRESSION?

Two rats are placed side by side in a gondola. They are tied down so that their range of movement is severely limited. An electric shock is administered to both, causing them to struggle. One of the pair is quite helpless and must suffer the pain regardless of how much it struggles. The other is luckier. If by chance a thrashing paw presses a switch the current will be turned off and both rats will have a brief respite from pain. Soon, however, the shock will be automatically or manually readministered and the torture will continue until the lucky rat again presses the switch. Rats are intelligent animals who learn quickly. Soon the lucky rat ties together the cessation of pain and the pressure on the switch and responds to the turning on of current by promptly turning it off again. Its life is still a sequence of short sharp shocks, but it is in control to at least the extent of having access to the switch.

That is why one rat is lucky. Its companion experiences the same shocks but unlike the lucky rat has no control. It may not understand, but it is completely dependent on its partner to stop his pain. That is why I keep calling the rat with its paw on the switch lucky. Lucky rats survive even in the psychology laboratory. Not so the rat who is helpless.

The lucky rat shows little sign of its trauma. Its coat remains sleek, its appetite good. When released it makes a quick and apparently full recovery from its ordeal. Not so the helpless rat. Its coat looks as if it has been liberally coated in cooking fat. It has no appetite. Freed from the round of torture it remains listless and depressed. Most die within a very short period. In summary, an animal who is submitted to torture dies not from the effects of the physical pain, but from the emotional pain of powerlessness.

Of course, you cannot extrapolate directly from rat to human being, so you perform another experiment. In this three groups of human subjects are used. Each is given a simple and similar task to perform which requires a modicum of concentration. Each is subjected to unpleasant noise. Like the lucky rat, one group has a switch and they can switch off the noise at will. The second group assumes the role of the unlucky rat in that they have no switch and must tolerate the noise whenever it is turned on. The third group, the control, have a switch and are told that they can turn off the noise if it becomes intolerable. They are asked, however, not to use the switch as to do so will 'spoil the experiment'.

The results are as follows:

● The 'lucky rat group' perform the task well and show no ill effects. Hardly surprising since they usually turn off the noise as soon as it is turned on.
● The 'unlucky rat' group perform badly and show severe signs of irritability and even depression, from which they take some time to recover.

● *The controls, who generally were subjected to the noise as much as were the 'unlucky rat' group and who did not exercise their option to switch it off, performed almost as well as the lucky rat team and showed no ill effects. This is dramatic confirmation that being potentially in control, even if you choose not to use your power, protects you from the worst effects of your environment and enhances performance even in difficult conditions.*

Depression is the loss of interest, creativity and the power to perform. In our society it follows hard on the heels of heart attack, cancer and stroke as a major killer. That is a strong argument for empowerment, self-regulating teams or self-directed teams. By giving power to the people it is possible to protect their emotional health, improve their performance and free their sometimes considerable creativity. This does not mean that there is a reduced role for the leader. Successful empowerment is a possibility. It may even become a necessity, but empowerment can only succeed in a disciplined environment. Empowerment requires super leadership.

SUPERLEADERSHIP – THE GOAL OF EVERY LEADER

Look again at the Lao Tsu quotation at the head of this chapter. It describes superleadership in action. This is 'empowerment' as it ought to be – committed teams achieving exceptional success under subtle and sensitive leadership.

In recent years empowerment has been one of the fads, fallacies, futilities and foul-ups which my friend Alistair Mant has attacked so cogently. What I call the 'let my people go' school of empowerment has claimed, on little or no evidence, that you have only to take all controls off people to release a flood of creativity and focused enterprise to the unbounded good of the organisation. They are wrong. What usually happens is that two very different behaviours emerge. One group, denied the leadership which they need, are paralysed. They know neither what they should do nor what they may do. They respond by doing as little as possible. This is a very sensible, though unproductive, way of minimising the short-term risk. It may also sting management into once again giving the leadership which most people need.

A second and usually smaller group turn liberty to licence. Denied constraints or guidance they try anything, no matter how eccentric, in an orgy of anarchic activity. This maximises risk, but not for them. The risk is strictly for the organisation which employs them. Sooner or later, usually later when the harm has been considerable, the brakes are applied. Now it is clear to all that management were merely playing games once again. There is another indicator of what I call the bus queue syndrome: 'Ignore this fad, there'll be another along in a moment!'

Empowerment, self-directed or self managed teams, call it what you will, can get extraordinary results from 'ordinary' people. To do so, however, does not require an abdication of management, it requires leadership of the highest order. It requires leaders who can coach for exceptional performance, identify when and by how much to let go, and who, while protecting the team from harm, never intrude on their ability to create their own success. Exceptional team performance starts and is sustained by exceptional leader performance, and that means subtle and strong influencing skills.

CHARACTERISTICS OF THE SUPERLEADER

Vision

The ability to develop and communicate a clear, exciting, challenging and motivating future for the team and for the business or community.

Charisma

At last this overused word comes into its own. In this case I am using it to mean the ability to inspire, influence and enable: the key attributes of the successful coach in sport, business or politics.

Customer commitment

Driven by free market ideologies we are no longer patients, passengers or colleagues, we are customers. That is fine as long as it leads to a real urge to listen and a desire to serve, rather than to meaningless charters and pointless targets. In a truly self-directed team we are all customers of each other and above all of the superleader. We want success. The superleader understands what we count as success and guides us to exceed our desires.

Quality focus

The superleader ensures that there is understanding of the level of
quality which will delight the external customer and differentiate the
firm in the marketplace. They then manage our personal growth
through life-long learning applied to the real world just in time. We
learn. We use what we have learned. We are rewarded and our
learning is reinforced. We seek to learn more.

Integrity

You cannot lie to a team and expect them to perform. You cannot lie to
a customer and expect repeat or referral business. There must be an
unequivocal commitment to honesty, even when the truth hurts in the
short term. Superleaders know when to keep their mouth shut perhaps,
but they are never economical with the truth or profligate with lies.

Accountability

Superleaders clearly define goals which are honest as well as being
rigorous. They neither ask for more than is reasonable in the hope of
squeezing out a little extra performance nor set easy targets to ensure
worthless success. All goals are clearly communicated. Responsibility
for achievement is delegated sensitively, but acountability for success
is retained where it belongs – with the leader.

Compassion and fairness

'Firm, but fair' ceases to be a meaningless catchphrase with the
superleader. Concern for the feelings of others motivates timely
support and help, but the realisation that success ultimately depends
on the right things being done in the right way at the right time means
that the superleader ensures that, one way or another, the team
carries no passengers. Tough decisions sometimes must be made.
When they are they are made on a timely basis. They are fair and
compassionate with regard to all the people involved and, most
importantly, the superleader takes absolute responsibility for the
decision and its ramifications.

Influence

Superleaders listen carefully and probe for new ideas and new concepts. They understand the needs of each individual in their team and work to show how those needs can best be realised through the achievement of shared objectives.

Principled

Martin Luther King said that anyone who had nothing that they would die for had nothing worth living for. Superleaders incorporate their values into the values of the team and team values into the values of the organisation – and they live them, all day, every day. As Americans say, they walk their talk.

Communication

Communication is an art form. Good communication is open, clear, concise, candid, complete, consistent and timely. It develops trust by earning trust, just as doing things together and succeeding build trust within the team. The role of reason and emotion in persuasive communication is understood and used in the interests of team success.

Risk taking

Leadership is a high-risk business. Superleaders study team dynamics and individual behaviour and use their knowledge to limit risk, but at the margin they trust people – and that is a high-risk strategy.

Ownership

Superleaders encourage the team to own both opportunities and problems. They own accountability for final outcomes and responsibility for coaching the team.

Coaching

The appropriate use of feedback which is timely and behaviour centred is directed at enabling team members to reach their full potential. Team members are taught to play their role as peer coaches and a true learning community is developed.

Awareness

Achievement is immediately recognised, acknowledged and rewarded. Superleaders always take the time to praise as readily as they take the time to redirect.

Intelligence

Always practical, always sensitive to present and future need, superleaders need to be intelligent, not intellectual.

Knowledge and skill

Superleaders believe in life-long learning not only for others, but for themselves. What they learn they freely pass to those who can use it.

Initiative

Superleaders look for and exploit opportunities for positive change. They create challenge which is in line with the growing ability of their team and use their influencing skills to create champions for change within and beyond the group.

Quick thinking

Competitive advantage in a volatile world is often dependent on speed of implementation. Superleaders understand this and use speed as a competitive weapon. They constantly hone their influencing skills to get decisions quickly and effectively implemented.

Global thinking

Superleaders value diversity and promote it within the team.

Parent, teacher, manager or salesperson, you are living in a world which increasingly demands that you become and remain a superleader. The greater the demand for democracy, the greater the need for leadership. People can and will deliver extraordinary results. They will not do so, however, through happenstance. People thrown in at the deep end have a great opportunity to drown.

The leader who recognises, fosters and releases talent so that confidence never outruns competence will bring the team to outstanding success. Having achieved success, the role of the leader is to plan and introduce new challenge so that the cycle of growth and success is constantly renewed. This is the challenge which ultimately all of us face.

SUMMARY

Research indicates that power is the key motive of the effective leader. This is not power for its own sake, but the constant search to get things done and get them done better through the guided efforts of others. Achievement and concern for the well-being of others are other important leadership motives, but the first must not be allowed to get in the way of the growth of others and the second must not be a barrier to making tough decisions.

Lack of power is a major cause, if not the only base cause, of clinical depression. Even suicide may be a last desperate attempt to take power in one's life.

Sources of power must be understood and power must be used congruently. Power is not to become a selfishly applied personal possession. It must be passed to others to the degree that is realistic given their maturity and motivation. This is most effectively achieved through self-directed teams and superleadership. This puts high demands on the leader, but it should be the goal of all influence professionals.

Influence and Psychology *11*

WHAT YOU WILL GAIN FROM THIS CHAPTER

- An understanding that practical approaches are more useful than ideologies
- The ability to draw useful lessons from even apparently conflicting sources
- Some ideas on how to reduce or avoid stress
- An opportunity to consider your values concerning the ethics of influencing another person's behaviour
- An understanding of the differences and similarities between the two major schools of psychology and how their concepts relate to the real world

---

Before enlightenment, chop wood – carry water. After enlightenment, chop wood – carry water.

Why can't a psychologist's parrot talk psychology?

(Mary Midgley)

I am by no means the only person to have long felt that some of the key concepts of Zen Buddhism are appropriate to business.

ZEN AND BUSINESS

First, Zen thought brings us back time and time again to the important practical activities of life. Second, and in the business world most important, Zen refuses to be dependent on faith. Zen has no ideology other than that of having no ideology. If businesspeople would reject the need for ideologies the purveyors of the fads, fallacies and foul-ups which so regularly send organisations into expensive sidetracks would enjoy slim pickings. Third, Zen is ethical and environmentally sound in the widest sense. Fourth, Zen is a way of life in which if there is a simpler way of doing things, that is the preferred way.

A Zen master was sitting by the shore when his reverie was interrupted by an excited monk.

'Master, master! After years of study I have walked on water. I have just walked across this lake!'

'Dear me, is there something wrong with the boat?'

Whose mind has set? A classic psychology experiment demonstrates the opposite of Zen in action. Imagine a perfectly ordinary living room with one minor exception. The room is furnished plainly with a few chairs and a side table. On the table is a vase containing a delightful bunch of spring flowers in water. On the floor in front of the table is a narrow glass tube, about a metre high, at the bottom of which a pingpong ball lies snugly. The tube, which has a sealed glass base, is fixed to the floor and cannot be lifted. Close to the tube are a number of long pieces of wire, some long-nosed pliers and other tools.

Subjects of the experiment are told only that their task is to remove the ball from the tube in the fastest possible time without damaging ball or glass in any way. Most people quickly find that the ingenious hooks and other tools which they have fashioned from the wire will not work. The ball fits too tightly. Since they are unable to raise the ball, none of the other tools are of any use.

Many subjects sweat and fume trying desparately to raise the ball. Very few walk the couple of steps to the table and tip water from the vase into the tube to make the ball float gently to the top from where it can be removed with any of the tools provided. The assumption that only the given tools are 'allowed' is just a mindset. Zen helps to rid us of this self-imposed disability.

I see the effect of mindsets regularly in my consultancy practice. When asked why they continue to do something that doesn't work and which clearly hasn't worked for years, managers often tell me that the rules require them to do it that way. If asked to show me the rule, they are often surprised to find that it doesn't exist. Sadly, without specific guidance there is no guarantee that the newly recognised absence of compulsion will lead to any change in behaviour.

Far beyond the walls of the psychology laboratory, mindset and habit combine to ensure that we fail to find the practical and simple solution to our problems.

Zen requires that solutions and the actions which they initiate should be simple, not simplistic. Anyone familiar with oriental calligraphy will recognise the sophistication which lies behind the simple line placed with one unerring stroke.

I mentioned the 'bus queue syndrome' in Chapter 10. This happens when the employees and management of any organisation have seen so many flavour-of-the-month fads introduced and then happily abandoned long before they have had time to work because another exciting gimmick has been promoted, that they make no attempt to make the current novelty work, comfortably aware that 'there'll be another one along in a minute'. Susceptibility to such fads is largely dependent on dogma.

Don't let someone's tale wag your dogma

When a manager tells me, with fervour, 'I believe in empowerment (or process reengineering, or whatever)', I tend to fear the worst. That is not to say that empowerment, process reengineering or anything else is inherently bad. It is simply that deep and disciplined thought based on critically appraised personal experience is often better. Maureen Lipman took great pride in her imaginary grandson having an 'ology', but if the only 'ology' you've got is an ideology, you'd be better off without it.

It is almost an ideology with Zen that it has no dogma. The teachings of Zen are a raft: useful when crossing water, but to be left behind when you reach the shore. Zen teaches us never to let what was once useful become a burden.

Zen is comprised of great faith, great doubt and great determination:

● Great faith in oneself, one's own personal experience and judgement.
● Great doubt in the sense of total absence of mindset.
● Great determination to achieve in the real world.

Before you study Zen, mountains are mountains and rivers are rivers. While you study mountains cease to be mountains and rivers cease to be rivers. But when you have enlightenment mountains are mountains and rivers are rivers again.

AROUSAL IS GOOD, STRESS IS BAD

In psychology there are two curves which dominate their relevant areas of thought. The *normal distribution* of most traits from height to assertiveness produces a bell shape curve when sufficient examples are transferred to a graph. Equally famous is the *Yerkes curve*.

This is an inverted U which demonstrates that learning and performance are relatively poor when arousal is low. Both improve as arousal increases to an optimal level, but performance and learning fall off as quickly as they increased once that arousal plateau is passed. Some psychologists have related stress with overarousal. Thus if I am blasé about giving a talk I will probably perform poorly. If I am somewhat nervous I will do much better. If I am paralysed with fear I will not be able to perform at all.

The late Hans Selye, a leading researcher into stress, coined the words understress, eustress and distress for what have become popularly known as 'rustout', arousal and 'burnout'. Eustress or arousal is, therefore, a good and necessary part of life: the excitement that I experience when facing a new challenge.

Understress and distress are equally destructive

We often seek to deal with understress by creating and indulging in behaviours which have no intrinsic meaning. As Mary Midgley puts it, 'activity for its own sake is a pattern which pervades human life'. Consider the UK's national winter game of football (soccer if you're American). No one would be happy just shooting balls into the net with a cannon. We make the game difficult simply to create arousal. In a similar vein, Masters and Johnson have shown the deleterious effect of regarding sex merely as a means to an orgasm. Payoff is not the key to satisfaction. Challenge and intimate warmth often are.

Stress is unavoidable – and stress in the form of eustress or arousal is desirable and often very enjoyable. What, then, is the difference between good and bad stress? Evolution works to a slow clock, cultural change is fast. The meme is faster than the gene.

In evolutionary terms the stress response prepares the body for fight or flight. If you are faced with a sabre-toothed tiger the ability to respond quickly and appropriately without thinking could mean the difference between living long enough to pass on your genes to a new generation and having your corpse, or what was left of it, left on the wasteground of development of the species. Even today such a response can save life.

There was a recent incident in the US in which a small girl was literally run over by a car. The toddler was carrying a teddy bear which miraculously wedged between her body and the underside of the car, saving her from being crushed. But a teddy bear under a ton and a half of car doesn't protect anybody for long. Fortunately a woman passerby, subject to stress at witnessing the accident and the child's plight, grabbed the car's bumper and raised the vehicle high enough to enable others to drag the child clear.

Superhuman performance in an emergency is what stress developed to facilitate, but superhuman performance is not called for most times when stress strikes.

Stress, if not used and dissipated, feeds on itself. The release of powerful chemicals into the system leads to the release of more and more in a circular and stress-building way. You have two choices.

You can either use stress as evolution intended – not an easy option in the office – or you can learn to manage it.

For many years it has been known that relaxation and complete concentration help to dispel stress. Many activities, from complex hobbies and vigorous sports to meditation and contemplation, exist to help to stressproof us, and I recommend that anyone seriously subject to stress explore the options with the aid of a good specialist text. But you can hardly be expected to start drawing or begin a tough game of squash if stress begins to build during a meeting or while trying to get fractious and lively children to bed. So try this Zen activity which works every time and which no one will notice that you are doing.

> 1. Close your eyes if the situation allows, if not look at a point downwards and a little in front of you.
> 2. Sit, or stand, as upright as possible.
> 3. Place your hands unobtrusively into a position where the palms face each other. If you're alone and unobserved place them in a loose facsimile of hands in prayer if that feels comfortable. If not, just rest the little finger edge of the hand on each thigh.
>
> And now comes the part which sounds daft, but which is, for those who practise it, relaxation magic.
>
> 4. Inhale as deeply as circumstances allow and as you do so imagine that the air is entering through the tips of your fingers.
> 5. Breathe out and feel – and I do mean feel – the air being released through your palms.
> 6. Take and release two or three further breaths, concentrating all the time on your finger tips with the inhalation and your palms as you exhale. As you do so you will find that your hands feel increasingly and pleasantly warm. What is more important, you will feel relaxed and better able to cope with the difficult customer, fractious child or impossible boss.

I learned that technique recently from an adept at oriental martial arts. Since learning it I have passed it on to others, who have invariably enjoyed the same satisfactory results. I am told, and since I lack access to an electroencephalograph I take their word for it, that this little-known technique puts the brain into slow alpha waves which create total relaxation and clarity of mind. Thus the brain signals that stress time is over and the vicious circle of stress is broken.

Frankly I don't care how it works. The important thing is that it works for me as it will work for you, and at heart, that is what Zen is all about.

ZEN AND ETHICS

In spite of the major changes in the structure of business which I outlined in Chapter 1, I believe that the key change which will have most effect in the long term is the renaissance of ethical behaviour in business and private life. Zen, not surprisingly, offers some relevant and useful thoughts on ethics.

Generosity	Keep the needs of others constantly at the forefront of your mind.	**SIX ZEN (AND LIFESTYLE) VIRTUES**
Morality	Avoid tricks and underhand approaches to influence. Rely instead on showing others, honestly, an infallible path to the satisfaction of their needs.	
Patience	Avoid short cuts and manipulation. Strive until you can get it right first time every time for all time.	
Vigour	Show a proper enthusiasm to serve others' needs, and look after yourself, physically, spiritually, and emotionally so that you may do so.	
Concentration	Decide where you need to go and go there. Be flexible about the route if circumstances demand it, but keep your thoughts on the goal and avoid unnecessary meandering.	
Wisdom	Do the right things today to serve your immediate necessary purposes, but never lose sight of the well-being of others or the future.	

**THE EIGHTFOLD
PATH**

Right views	Give primacy to the other person's point of view as it is, rather than as you wish it to be.
Right intentions	Achieve your goals through helping others to achieve theirs.
Right speech	Take care with structure, sequence and content, making the other's need fulfilment the centre of your discourse.
Right action	Learn all that you can and remember that learning has not taken place until you turn skill and knowledge into action.
Right livelihood	Believe in what you are trying to do. If what you have to do makes you unhappy or unfulfilled, put everything that you have at the service of finding something different. As my friend Adrian Furnham says: 'Work must be more fun than fun.'
Right effort	Put in no more effort than is needed to achieve your goals and learn better ways so that the required effort reduces over time.
Right mindfulness	Discipline the mind and the tongue to influence the behaviour of others economically and honestly.
Right concentration	On mutually beneficial outcomes of behaviour. Create your world in which win/win is the norm.

ZEN AND PSYCHOLOGY

Psychology can be defined as the study of cognition (thinking, perceiving and remembering), emotion and behaviour. Arguably, since thinking, perceiving and remembering are all activities or behaviours, the definition could be reduced to the study of emotion and behaviour, but I believe, contrary to what the behaviourists say, that the mind cannot be reduced to an irrelevant black box and so I prefer the fuller definition.

The study of human behaviour and human nature is probably as old as mankind itself. Certainly the ancient Greeks and in particular Aristotle had much to say on the subject. But in 1879 in Leipzig a physiologist, Wilhelm Wundt, set up the first psychology laboratory. Wundt and his followers were called structuralists because they suggested that complex mental activities were built from a simple mental state – and therein lies the rub. Once you give a dog a name you can declare it bad and you give yourself an excuse to hang it.

There is a human tendency to believe that our way is the only way and that everything that predates is or challenges it must be wrong, intellectually dishonest and therefore hateful. Sometimes science in general and psychology in particular seem to seek to advance by clinging to the patently untrue in the face of the promising, and throwing what might otherwise be thriving infants out with the barely dirty bathwater. So each school of psychology – functionalists, gestaltists, behaviourists and so on – rejects the work of those who preceded them.

NATURE VERSUS NURTURE AGAIN

A silly fight which has spread its shadow further than common sense would think possible is the quarrel between those who proselytise a religion that all behaviour is x per cent dependent on evolution and therefore, being part of our genetic endowment, cannot be changed; and those, equally driven by an ideology, who believe that the environment rules to the extent of at least y per cent, as a result of which we are infinitely malleable.

Behaviour is dictated in part by our genetic endowment and in part by our upbringing, but to try to establish that it is x per cent this and y per cent that is as productive as estimating the number of angels who can dance on the head of a pin. Let me give you a serious example of why it's a daft argument.

There is a genetic condition called phenylketonuria (PKU). The condition is a serious one which among its nastier tricks can produce congenital feeblemindedness. This is a totally genetic condition which occurs only when a child receives two recessive genes, one from each of its parents, and in no other way. The immediate effect of inheriting this genetic booby trap is that the child is unable to use the important amino acid phenylalanine which is a common constitute of a number of foods.

If the breakdown of phenylalanine is blocked, toxins accumulate in the body and, unless the problem is identified and resolved before the patient is six months old, irreversible brain damage occurs. If the condition is recognised, however, treatment is simple and completely effective. The patient is put on a diet low in phenylalanine and normal mental development occurs.

So we have a situation in which a rare (1 in 10,000) and extreme genetic condition is totally controllable by environmental means. Control the diet and save the child.

Environment and genetic endowment are always mixed to some degree. Nature and nurture blend so that in most cases it is impossible to see the join – so where is the sense in trying to divide x per cent of one from y per cent of the other?

Small changes in belief, attitude or behaviour by a large number of people can change culture several times in a single lifetime. But although cultural change rapidly outdistances biological change, it can never move too far away from it. Societies in which genetic endowment leads to the development of a culture which is self-destructive, apathetic or otherwise dangerous will leave less successors and others, more constructive and more enthusiastic, will prevail. In the long term biology triumphs. Organisms develop in appropriate cultures or they die.

Often we have little idea of what is cultural and what is inherited. Charles Darwin had a way of extrapolating difficult problems from ordinary situations. If blushing is, as it seems to be, some sort of social signal, do those of us who are prone to blush do so only on those parts of their bodies which are not covered by their clothes, or does the blusher turn 'pinky pink all over' like Piglet? He appealed to his medical friends for advice. They informed him that certainly many carefully raised young women blush when faced with an intimate medical examination requiring them to remove some or all of their clothing. Equally certainly, the extent of the blush is limited to face, throat and shoulders, those parts of the body visible when they are normally clad.

This raises the interesting question: is blushing a matter of evolution or culture? Genetic phenomenon or cultural convention? If the tendency to blush is inherited with our genes, is it not a delightful thought that evolution appears to have accurately predicted the depths to which Victorian necklines would sink?

E.O. Wilson, whose wonderful book *On Human Nature* created a new science of sociobiology, put it more succinctly than I can hope to:

> Rather than specify a single trait human genes prescribe the capacity to develop a certain array of traits. In some categories of behaviour the categories are limited and the outcome can be altered only by strenuous training – if ever. In others, the array is vast and the outcome easily influenced.

REAL WORLD VERSUS LABORATORIES

A major reason for the unattractive infighting which has dogged psychology is the admirable concern which some professionals have demonstrated to ensure that their area of study is truly scientific. Some psychologists want psychology to be a 'hard science' like physics. This view has driven psychology away from the mind into the laboratory to study behaviour. That's fine as far as it goes. Laboratory experiments have provided valuable insights. But there is much more to life than can be seen in laboratories, no matter how carefully designed the experiment.

The purpose of laboratory work in general is to enable the study of specific, usually measurable behaviours under conditions of absolute control. The intention is to have unambiguous, reliable, properly quantified results.

Yet for all the careful and valuable work that is done in laboratories, is it possible to maintain a squeaky clean scientism? I doubt it. Experiments are done on people or on other mammals or birds. If the subject is non-human, can the results be extrapolated to tell us anything about human behaviour? The answer is sometimes 'yes' and sometimes 'no', but the problem is that you don't need many 'nos' to enable one group to start calling another 'ratologists'.

Do we need to worry that psychology is not absolute but statistical? That is, does it matter that the findings are true of most people most of the time rather than all people all of the time? Not if you want it to be like physics. I'm no physicist, but I understand enough to be clear that physics is statistical too. Go poking around for an electron and you can predict with some accuracy where you will find it, but if you really do look for it don't expect it to be there. For any probability of it being found in one place there is a greater or lesser probability of it being found elsewhere.

Or consider the half-life of radioactive substances. For a given lump of uranium in a little more than 5000 years exactly half of it will have emitted particles through radioactivity and will have decayed to thorium. Exactly half to be sure, but no one knows which atoms will decay. It's a quantum sweepstake in which half of the tickets are winners and half are losers, but we only know which is which after the event.

When Einstein was developing the Special Theory of Relativity he considered the invariant speed of light by day dreaming as his bus moved away from Bern Town Hall that if the bus were to fly away from the clock tower at the speed of light he would be able to look back at the clock and see time stand still as the light rays merely kept pace with him. Hard science? Well yes, hard science that has been vindicated by all real world predictions which have been tested since 1905. I suspect that psychology should feel itself free to use laboratories when they suit its purpose and, at the extreme, sit on a bus and dream when that appears to be the better way. As long as the scientific method is respected there is nothing to worry about.

The scientific method requires that one should:

● observe reality
● form a theory

- make predictions based on the theory
- test the predictions through more observation
- revise the theory if necessary and retest

I believe that the vast majority of psychologists, whatever their school or the detail of their methodology, respect and work within the scientific method. Magpie that I am I choose to steal from all the predictive theories which have worked out in practice. I do so with gratitude, but with no allegiance to any 'ism'.

Zen teaches us that we have two eyes placed at the front of our heads. Either, in the normally sighted person, is able to provide a stream of valuable information with the other shut. Together, however, they give full depth to the picture and enable remarkable acts of skill and judgement. This is the Zen approach to psychology. Each school has made and is making a valid, valuable and limited contribution. One day someone will put all of the pieces together and we will see the whole picture. For me that really will be enlightenment.

THE ROLE OF BELIEF

Zen appeals to me, among other reasons, because it is adamant in rejecting dogma and blind faith. But what is the role of belief, justified or otherwise, in the management of behaviour?

Belief is omnipotent. Patients who believe in their doctors get better. Armies who believe in their generals achieve victory. What you believe you can do you will do. More to the point, when you set out to do things that you believe in and which you believe you can achieve, you will be unstoppable. Hold strongly to your beliefs and believe, above all things. in yourself, but remember the simple philosophy of the old wartime song which demanded that we 'praise the lord – and pass the ammunition'.

Don't expect belief to do it on its own. Faith alone may be able to move mountains, but faith allied with the right technology will do a better job more quickly.

SUMMARY

Zen is not a religion, it is a way of using the mind which emphasises practicality combined with morality. As such, it is worthy of study by all businesspeople.

Psychology is a science. Like all sciences it is statistical and subject to new discovery and the ultimate rejection of old theories when they are no longer deemed to be useful. Newtonian physics may be wrong, but as long as it is capable of sending men to the moon and getting them back, it is useful. The teachings of psychology may sometimes fail with the umteen millionth individual for reasons which are too complex to identify. That doesn't make it any more wrong than physics. It makes people even more interesting and the study of their behaviour ever more rewarding.

Forward to the Future 12

When asked recently on television whether there was not something worth salvaging from the economic philosophies pursued by the mainstream British political parties, Sir James Goldsmith replied:

> When their thinking is fundamentally flawed there is no point in rooting around to find something worth salvaging.

He was right in two vital ways.

To the trained the question sounds like a fundamental ploy of compliance psychology. If you want to beguile someone into weakening and finally destroying their own case, start with a small, apparently innocuous area of agreement. (Remember the Chinese and the subversion of American prisoners during the Korean War?) I don't know if Brian Walden is a student of psychology, but he is an astute and subtle interviewer and he may have been seeking that crucial self-inflicted wound which, if worked on assiduously, leads to a haemorrhage of reason.

Conversely his question may have been free of any hidden agenda. Similarly, I don't know whether Sir James answered as he did consciously avoiding a perceived pitfall, or whether he simply said what he knew to be true.

The existing politicians, snouts in the trough, are creating in the developed world new levels of wealth and poverty. In Great Britain and America today three out of five children are born into poverty, while the number of millionaires doubles each year. Real earnings of the wealth producers in America have fallen by almost 20 per cent.

Politicians assure us that the economy is improving by leaps and bounds. The majority of people grow poorer as the indices move higher. Goldsmith argues that the only possible purpose of the national economy is to enrich the lives of the population. As we enrich the few we so impoverish our societies that, in Faith Popcorn's striking word, the affluent are cocooning.

Popcorn is one of the highest paid and best respected consultants in the world. She paints two contrasting pictures of our future. She makes it clear that the choice is ours. In a world in which people of good will can be linked instantaneously by technology, we can work together to build the world that we choose, but there are two basic requirements:

- We must decide what kind of world we want and be prepared to work for it.
- We must develop the skills to bring others along with us.

That is why I believe that the skills in this book have an importance beyond the ordinary. You may choose to use them or you may want to resist them, but you need to understand them.

Before you think that I have taken leave of my usual feet on the ground approach and am suffering from delusions of grandeur, let me make clear why I think they are important using Faith Popcorn's two scenarios.

- *We could be living in a world where you literally can't open your door because of the piled-up garbage which costs too much to remove. As toxic waste builds up cities need to be evacuated. To slow down the poisoning of our environment we are barred from driving our cars more than three days a week. Most of us suffer because air-conditioning, now an essential, is owned as a monopolistic franchise which few can afford. Even a bath is a metered luxury which we can seldom justify unless we are very rich. When our children go to school they no longer run carelessly in the street. They* *are accompanied by an armed guard. Even adults rarely go out alone – it isn't safe. If you are rich enough you may kid yourself that you are enjoying the countryside by paying to join a fortified, closed and exclusive park. America is now a third-rate power, the UK is on a level with Haiti. The rich are rich prisoners who fear to go out into the world. The poor die on the streets. Costs of production of $16 an hour (America) and $12 an hour (UK) couldn't compete in a world in which the politicians scrambled for the non-existent free market and China, using prison labour, dominates the world with labour costs of cents, not dollars…*

● *Or we could have adopted a consume/replenish approach which means that we are no longer robbing our own children of their inheritance. Consumers and corporations share a determination to sustain a worthwhile ecology. Increasingly, people are developing socially and environmentally responsible businesses which they run from home using networks of electronic systems. Communities have gone back to the old ways. Things are shared, work is shared and people learn again that you can rely on your neighbours. Drugs, crime and poverty still exist, but the whole community works together to tackle the problems, with corporations living out their good neighbour claims by funding and resourcing education and social needs. The disadvantaged are assured of fair opportunities to earn a decent living. At work old game management has finally been genuinely superceded by new game management. True participation takes place when it's appropriate, the dumb 'let my people go' gurus have retired to their ivory towers, and business uses intelligent and humane methods because they work. There is a new respect for the individual and a new understanding of the role of the team. The high-income countries lead the world in quality products and transfer technology to the third world to produce high-quality, desirable goods which those who make them can afford to buy. Creative talent is recognised and we have civilised capitalism for the benefit of all. Values are those of which my granny would have approved, and values and a sense of direction are broadly shared…*

The trends, and Popcorn is the mistress of the trend, point at either scenario and, as I said, the choice is ours. Read the *Popcorn Report*, think it through and make your decision: then put your dreams to work. Help make people, all people, count again.

This book contains the information you need to make you a superinfluencer. How you use this information is for you alone to decide, but I hope this brief chapter will encourage you to take and use these skills to rebuild a better world for your children and for mine.

Workbook:
Building Your Skills

When I conduct short seminars I try to ensure the transfer of learning by making myself available to participants after the programme by telephone. This means that during a time when they are putting the ideas into effect I can support their efforts with further explanation and advice. Since frequent telephone communication with the tens of thousands who will read this book is not practical, it is necessary to design a different approach to the transfer of learning.

What follows is a step-by-step resumé of much of the information in the main part of this book. As such, it briefly outlines all that is currently known about influence and sales psychology. It offers a total game plan which, if applied with sensitivity and skill, will give you all that you desire from life.

Understand that from this moment you cannot fail. If you believe in yourself and you use all the skills which this book will give you, failure is no longer possible. Knowing that you cannot fail, you have total confidence in your own ability. Fear of failure, like fear of rejection is for you a thing of the past. When you decide on your future objectives always bear in mind the basis on which they are set. *They are based on your ability to achieve whatever goals you totally commit yourself to achieving.* Not by magic or by wishful thinking, but by the application of proven psychological strategies. This book explains to you the findings of science which, flexibly and sensitively used, ensure success. The workbook summarises the key concepts of the book for quick reference. It is designed to help turn reading into action.

The question 'What would you seek to do if you knew that you could not fail?' is a relevant one for you to consider. Remember, I am not offering you a miracle cure. I am not about to suggest that if you daydream enough what you seek will come to you. Some of what I suggest will come easy, some will require committed and enjoyable effort. The important thing is that there is a comprehensive body of research which clearly identifies what works. If you learn and practise the skills in this book, you will succeed in all that you want to do. If you are wise you will work hard at what you will turn into creative play. With this book you will get where you want to go and you will enjoy the journey.

Knowing that, write below whatever honestly and seriously comes to your mind – do it now.

My key objectives today are:

```



```

I will succeed because I will:

```



```

Decide that from today, regardless of your past experience, concerns or doubts, you are a superb communicator.

In sales and management situations a superb communicator is simply one who listens effectively. To listen effectively you need to concentrate on four things. You want to know:

● What the other person thinks and feels
● What the other person needs and wants
● The most important want which the other person has right now
● What problems, real or potential, stand between the other and the achievement of their goals today.

Repeatedly research shows that the effective sales communicator *listens* at least 60 per cent of the time in all sales situations. To listen for long periods with the same level of intensity is not difficult – it is impossible. You need to learn and practise 'in–out' listening. This means that you listen intently until you hear something which demands a response from you. That response may be in the form of a very brief written note, a comment or even a simple nod of comprehension and agreement. The action is enough to give your brain a brief break, allowing you to tune in again to what is being said without fatigue. Remember that the brain processes information and remembers by making connections. By actively making connections in what you hear you will remember better and be able to listen effectively for long periods if necessary.

Although listening, the sales or management communicator always controls the conversation to ensure that they get the information which they want.

To listen and control the situation you need to ask questions, but you need to do much more than that. You must control the flow of information from the other person.

In the early stages of the conversation you need to maximise the flow of information so that the barriers come down and the other person genuinely tells you what they think and how they feel about things.

Think about and write down some typical questions which will get you the information you need to succeed.

Question:

Why I ask this question, what information I expect to elicit:

Question:

Why I ask this question, what information I expect to elicit:

Question:

Why I ask this question, what information I expect to elicit:

To maximise the flow of conversation you must:use *open* questions which cannot be answered by a 'yes' or a 'no' and which cause the other person to express their feelings or opinion:

- 'How do you feel about the state of the economy at present?'
- 'Did you hear the President's speech last night? What did you think?'
- 'What are the most significant values that you as a businessperson hold?'

But asking open questions is not enough – you must reward the other person for giving you valuable information by:

- Thanking them: 'That's very interesting, thank you.'
- Praising them: 'You're very generous (kind, brave, honest…) sharing that with me.'
- Smiling and making eye contact.
- Nodding.
- Paraphrasing key ideas to show that you are listening.
- Asking for further information: 'That's very interesting. Could you tell me a little more about that?'
- Maintaining an alert and interested posture.
- Asking further 'open' questions.

Use more focused or semi-closed questions to increase your control of the conversation, reduce meandering and garrulousness, and clarify your own thinking. These are questions which clearly indicate the area which you want the other person to address without demanding a short or 'yes/no' answer:

- 'Why is it a problem particularly to you?'
- 'Why is that so important at the moment?'
- 'What have you tried within the last year to achieve the outcome that you are looking for?'
- 'What would be your ideal solution?'

Closed questions

When you have all the information you need, or are likely to get, turn up the control mechanism another notch by asking genuinely closed questions.

- 'The redundancy programme is the only area where you want to hear my ideas right now?'
- 'Do you have a budget for this?'
- 'Is your key objective to reduce downtime by 20%?'

Absolute control comes from asking questions to which the only reasonable answer is 'yes'.

Value questions

- 'As a parent, do you agree that the quality of education will be critical to your child's future?'
- 'Do you agree that we who have so much should do what we can to reduce the suffering of starving children?'

Leading questions

- Having satisfied you on all the points you've raised, do you think it might be a good idea?'
- 'Do you see why short-term growth is the right strategy in today's conditions?'

To keep your argument on track once you are doing a considerable share of the talking and to keep the other actively involved, use:

Progress test questions

- 'Have I made it clear how the new system will solve your problems?'
- 'Does what I've said (shown you, given you a feel for) help. Does it sound (look, feel) right to you?'

Obstacle handling questions

- 'Yes that does sound difficult, if I can show you how to overcome that will we have a deal?'
- 'Is that your only concern?'

BIOLOGICAL FACTORS REVIEWED

Your brain can take in at least one hundred million 'bits' of information every second. To all intents and purposes its capacity is infinite. Imagine how it would be if we were consciously aware of all the information which we receive. We would be overwhelmed trying to consider it all and we would become incapable of making a decision and totally unable to take even the simplest action.

For our distant ancestors, living in the wild among predators, such an incapacity would have ensured early and violent death. Evolution has therefore provided us with a filtering system which pushes most information directly into our unconscious mind while enabling us to be aware of essential facts.

The downside is that we respond to these key facts automatically in what biologists call the 'click-whirr' response – and the information, being partial, is often misleading.

Professional persuaders understand this and they ensure that the appropriate partial cues are always expressed in every situation in which they choose to exert influence over others.

The cues leading to the 'click-whirr' response are:

CONSISTENCY

We are always want to act consistently with our expressed beliefs and values. This extends into the area of whether we are likely to keep our word after entering into an agreement. If I believe that I have been genuinely party to developing the terms of an agreement, rather than railroaded into it, I am more than three times as likely to stick to my side of the bargain even when the 'bargain' turns out to be a burden.

Trainers, salespeople, consultants and change agents who know their business all tell their clients, customers and colleagues to decide on their goals and 'write them down'. Why the insistence on the writing? Because research shows and experience confirms that the act of writing something down of itself increases commitment considerably. If you are ever asked by a salesperson to fill out the order yourself, it is with good (though not necessarily ethical) reason. Because you wrote it you are very unlikely to cancel it – even when you discover it is not the good deal you thought. Instead you will internalise and emphasise all the reasons why it appeared to be a great opportunity and downplay or ignore all arguments to the contrary.

Beware the effect of offering or giving large rewards for behaviour consistent with commitments. Strangely, the offering or application of a large reward is counterproductive for two main reasons. First, and most important, it dilutes the commitment by providing a competing motivation for the behaviour. Second, it denies the individual ownership of the behaviour. Rewards are important in many situations, but all scientists researching the effects have tended to the view that the reward must be the minimum which is consistent with the desired outcome.

Behaviour is moulded and reinforced most effectively by small rewards frequently repeated, and for most of us much of the time the internalised reward of sticking to our beliefs and behaving consistently with them is enough.

FRIENDSHIP

We like to acquire something new, but we do not like to be sold to by slick salespeople. If the salesperson can assume the role of 'friend' it will be extremely difficult to reject them and their product.

The friendship concept lies at the base of the sales referral. It is not always easy to build a positive relationship with the potential customer sufficiently quickly to ensure favourable attention. The next best thing is for the salesperson to present themself as the 'friend of a friend'. From door to door household goods sales through cars to services such as consultancy, the ability to say 'Joe sent me' is a valued way to ensure a positive hearing.

Sales manuals suggest that the referral is 50 per cent of the sale. They may be wrong – it may be rather more than that. Not only does the referral practically guarantee a hearing, if you reject the salesperson you reject your friend's opinion that you would profit from the product. It also ensures in most cases that competitors are not in the frame, and that there is a perceived need and the salesperson is the friend who can fill that need.

To survive in a competitive world we need to cooperate and build relationships. In practice we have developed an internal drive to go one step further. We repay favour not just with favour, but with interest.

That is nature's way of assisting our survival by putting the rest of the world a little in our debt. If favour begets favour we are on an upward cycle of mutual support, which is likely to be broken only in the most extreme circumstances where the other sees their very existence as being threatened.

We need to be accepted into the tribe to survive, we need to feel part of a group.

In psychology there is a basic law of relationships called the *paradigm of exchange*: in human relations any relationship is likely to be maintained as long as the costs of maintenance are less than the benefits received by each party.

In conditions of certainty social validation is neither necessary or useful, but in periods of uncertainty and confusion social validation will be sought and, if necessary invented, to bolster wished for 'truths'.

To get action in an apathetic group, reduce uncertainties in the following way:

- Make and maintain eye contact with one person
- Address that one person unambiguously by name or description
- Demand action from that one person
- After the desired action is taken, reinforce it with thanks, praise or reward

If uncertainties remain, group inaction will be reinforced by apparent social validation.

SOCIAL VALIDATION

A harsh natural environment taught us, through our genes, to grab for scarce resources. By definition scarce resources are unlikely still to be around if we hesitate, and our culture has designed the ultimate deal for the acquisition of scarcity. We have developed a society which enables us through hire purchase, credit cards etc. to 'grab now and pay later'.

It has long been known to marketing professionals that an effective way to boost sales from a direct mail piece is as follows:

SCARCITY

- Stage One: Telephone the prospect in advance of the mailing and 'sell' them on reading it.
- Stage Two: Follow the mailing with a second telephone call.

The prospect will almost certainly have fulfilled their undertaking to read the piece. Further. they will have justified to themselves their reasons for doing so by finding something of value in what they have read. What is more, they will have shifted their perception of themselves further toward the 'open-minded' end of their perceptual continuum. Lastly, in thinking about the product or service offered they will have built a case in their minds for acquiring it.

In short, you have a patsy eager to buy. So at stage two you sell, right? Most salespeople do and their sales are high.

But if you are a junk investment salesperson you don't and you take it all. You thank the prospect for their interest and explain that demand to invest has been so immense that you are unable to take instructions at this time. Thus you add the missing ingredients of scarcity and denial of an assumed freedom to your mark. Later, and not too much later – you don't want your victim to come to terms with his perceived loss – you call again, breathless and excited. An unexpected opportunity to sign up a very limited number of new investors has occured. He can get in on the act, but only if he acts now and invests a minimum sum. Click-whirr goes into action. The investor parts with his savings and another offshore scam is considerably richer while the investor is very much poorer.

Physiological response to alleged scarcity have been measured. People show clear symptoms of stress, panic and aggression when they believe themselves to be competing for a scarce resource.

AUTHORITY

Expert opinion carries enormous weight. A knowing salesperson will often provide a 'unbiased, expert report' to prospective buyers.

What makes this more powerful is that given the opportunity and the information to build our own case for acquiesence we build one which is more compelling and more targeted than any salesperson can hope to develop. Access to expert opinion allows us to make such a case in our own minds based on what we believe to be the unbiased facts. Evolution and culture have combined to create specialists, and we listen to them to save time and effort.

PSYCHOLOGY

More than 60 years of practical, carefully validated and comprehensive research have led to the development of a cognitive map of exactly – step by step – how people think when making a decision (see Figure 4.1 on page 45). Each step implies a question. If the presentation of your product, service or idea is structured so that each question is answered affirmatively in turn, the mind is programmed to reach the decision 'yes'. Only by inputting ideas at the wrong time or in the wrong sequence do we fail. Get the sequence and timing precisely right every time and you succeed every time.

Please note that the sequence, emotional climate and the actual words used are important.

PLANNING

If you want to succeed every time, commit yourself to planning. Most enterprises which fail do so because plans were incomplete or avoided. Most attempts at persuasion which founder do so for the same reason. To plan is to succeed, but as the old saying has it, 'those who fail to plan, plan to fail.'

The order in which you develop your plan is unlikely to be the order in which you speak. You can produce your plan in whatever sequence is easy for you, but the elements and the order in which they are expressed are absolutely dictated by the way that your 'listener' thinks. The sequence is the same for all normal brains. If you want to be successful all the time in the persuasion business you *must* present your ideas in the right sequence and with the right timing (see Figure 4.2 on page 46).

The first thought that you are likely to have if you plan systematically is the present 'buyer' behaviour which you want to change. For example they may:

● buy from your competitor Bloggs and Co

or:

● spend 40 minutes in the bathroom every morning, when you are anxious to get ready for an early appointment

or:

● smoke, drink or take drugs

or even:

● undervalue the potential of sales training

The first thing to notice is that if you are seeking to change behaviour it is essential that you think specifically about what the person is doing, not what they are failing to do. There is no such thing as a 'behavioural vacuum'. When others are not doing as you would wish, they are always doing something which can be changed to the desired behaviour. To be an effective change agent you must understand what that 'something else' is.

If you decide that it is essential to talk to them about their current and undesirable behaviour you must remember a few important rules:

● The way that I behave has been conditioned by its being useful in the past. I will therefore, with reason, be attached to my old habits and behaviours.
● If you confront me about my valued behaviour, whatevever it is, I will become defensive and you will have an uphill struggle to gain my favourable attention.
● You will be wise, therefore, not to mention my behaviour at all – but if you think that circumstances make some mention of my behaviour unavoidable you will:
● Avoid direct confrontation by 'depersonalising'. Never say 'you' – prefer a more neutral phrase such as: 'People who do…' It's weak, but it's all you have to work with if you want to avoid conflict.
● If you use a depersonalised approach, avoid expressing any problems that my behaviour may cause me as absolutes.
  Don't say: 'People who smoke will die of heart or lung disease.' I only need one counter example to launch into an argument, and an argument is what you must avoid if you wish to convince me.

Think of a behaviour of someone close to you that you might wish to persuade them to change.

PRACTICE
OPPORTUNITY

Behaviour:

```
[                                                              ]
```

Ill effects which I know that the behaviour does, or at some time will, cause the other:

```
[                                                              ]
```

An important goal which will be denied my 'cared for other' as a direct result of continuing the behaviour:

```
[                                                              ]
```

How I might raise the matter with my 'cared for other' if I thought it necessary to confront them over this behaviour:

```
[                                                              ]
```

Check:

Have I convincingly 'depersonalised'?   Yes ☐ No ☐

Have I plausibly 'neutralised'?   Yes ☐ No ☐

If I were to use the precise words as written above, could I realistically expect to avoid an argument?   Yes ☐ No ☐

Unless the answer to all three of the questions above is an unequivocal 'yes', don't risk it. Use one of the other techniques described in the book.

Say instead: 'People who smoke may die from painful and incapacitating lung or heart diseases.' No one sane can argue with that.

Mood and manner

The mood and manner which you adopt are often critical to the outcome of your efforts to influence others.

The best mood and manner to bring to an influencing situation is one which is close to that of your listener without being exaggerated, insensitive or tainted by cheap mimicry. In short, you must always be yourself, but if the other person is feeling quiet and serious be quiet and serious with them. Do not attempt in the early stages to change their mood by false bonhomie or wild enthusiasm. If they are brisk and businesslike, so are you.

If the other is miserable, you are serious and quiet, but don't burst into tears or exaggerate your behaviour in any way. That would be insensitive and stupid.

OTHER PEOPLE'S GOALS

Ironically, if you want to persuade me to do anything, *my goals and not yours* must be central to your approach and always in the forefront of your mind.

Assume that you have called by appointment to see me. I apologise, but I have to postpone our meeting.

I must get to the airport immediately to take an unplanned flight. I have just received a call that my father is dying. I hesitate briefly as I reach the door.

'Before I go can you just tell me in 10 seconds what you wanted to see me about? I'll think about it in the plane and we'll talk again when I return.'

You, following the advice in most textbooks, try to get out of telling me anything and insist that you will contact me on my return. Good move, but there's a better one.

Convince me that what you want to talk about is totally in my interest to hear and I *will* call you on my return.

The psychological advantage of having me invite you to call is immense. Go for it.

Tell me what I want to hear. In short, tell me convincingly that you want to talk to me about how I can achieve an objective dear to my heart. Most people fail at this hurdle by being excessively vague:

'I want to explain how you can save some money.'

Unconvincing, I've heard that too often from those who want me to spend, and go on spending with them. To make it work you have to say something very specific:

'I think I can see how you can increase your retained gross income by a minimum of 50 per cent.'

That's better. You now have until I get back and call you to do some more homework to test your good idea and prove that it will deliver what you've promised. But you're in the driving seat. Unless I think you a total idiot I will call and when you next visit me you will be perceived as an expert who is doing me a favour by coming to see me.

Goals come in two varieties: generic and specific.

Generic goals are those which all people having a specific role are almost certain to share. They are to be used when you have no opportunity to establish specific personal goals. Examples of generic goals might be:

Generic goals

Role	Goal
Businessperson	Enhanced return on funds employed
Entrepreneur	Potentially profitable business opportunity
Worker	Greater job satisfaction with less hassle
Salesperson	Easier, more profitable sales

Specific goals are those which are more personal. They are often far more important to the listener. You must never guess at these. They can only be established safely by skilful questioning

Specific goals

and careful listening. Some are so personal that even if you know about them it would be seen as a gross impertinence for you to offer help to attain them.

Sensitivity, as I have said before, is vital.

To establish and use goals

> • List all that the listener is prepared to share with you.
> • Deduce unexpressed goals by examining the listener's past behaviour and intelligently asking yourself, 'What were they trying to achieve?"
> • Test any goals which you are unsure of by using clarifying questions: 'Is improving revenues the most important factor at present?'
> • Clear from your mind and erase from your notes any goal which you have the slightest reason to feel might embarrass or annoy the listener if you were to pursue it.
> • Identify the most important goal which your product, service or idea can achieve and base your whole presentation on the achievement of that goal.
> • All subgoals which will be achieved en route to the main goal are important benefits.
> • To ensure that you are always working on the most powerful goal which your product, service or idea can attain, ask yourself, 'Why would they want that?' – and keep going until you come to the end of the logical sequence.
> • Take nothing for granted and make no assumptions. Listeners' goals are the cornerstone of your ability to influence. Ask progress test questions whenever you're in doubt.

Some managers and salespeople worry about asking progress test questions too often:

'Won't I look a bit of an idiot if I keep asking things like "Am I right in believing that XYZ is of importance to you right now?"'

The answer is that you will look a fool if and only if:

• You don't listen, and ask questions which have already been clearly answered.
• You work so rigidly to a formula that you automatically blurt

out the same words each time you ask a question. Some
people develop a formula for questions and most others find
it irritating. Make your questions sound natural.

What will make you seem really stupid, however, is if you put
together a brilliant presentation of how your idea will help gain
an objective which the other person is unconcerned about, or
which will solve a problem they don't have.

I see that happen frequently, particularly with managers,
parents or salespeople who start by rubbing their hands and
saying:

'Have I got a great idea for you!'

Of course, if your idea, product or service will not give the
listener their heart's delight, you have to make the best of what
it will do. The goal which can be achieved may not be the
greatest, but if you can *prove* that it will be achieved
economically, you will still succeed.

Work on only one principal goal at a time. You may hold the
key to solving every problem and meeting every goal that the
listener has or has ever dreamed of. Hold your fire and avoid
confusing your listener or blowing your credibility by appearing
to claim too much. The path must be shown to be straight, clear,
unbroken and logical to the achievement of the best you can
offer.

Once you have built your credibility you can indulge yourself
by showing the listener in a little more detail what a great idea
they have just bought. That will remove doubts and reinforce
the good decision to 'buy'.

Earlier you were asked to do some work with a behaviour of
someone close to you that you would like to change. Let's do
some more work on it.

To persuade someone to change their behaviour you need to
identify goals which they really care to attain and which the new
behaviour will *certainly* enable them to achieve. So an important
part of the planning process after you have identified the
behaviour you wish to see changed, and the behaviour which
will replace it, is to analyse the other's known goals.

Goals which I am certain my listener wants to achieve:

```
                                                   
                                                   
                                                   
```

My evidence for claiming that these are important:

```
                                                   
                                                   
                                                   
                                                   
```

Order of priority which my listener would give to their goals:

```
1.
2.
3.
4.
5.
6.
```

My evidence for this:

```
                                                   
                                                   
                                                   
```

Highest priority goal(s) which my idea can deliver:

```
                                                   
                                                   
                                                   
```

Do I have a good idea (product, service) for this person?

Yes ☐ No ☐

If 'no', how can I better tailor my idea to their need?

```
                                                   
                                                   
                                                   
```

Earlier it was argued that all the known evidence points to the unwisdom of confronting anyone to whom you are trying to sell, or whom you are seeking to influence, with their present undesirable behaviour. Our behaviour is reinforced only by its own success. My past behaviour has made me what I am today and whatever that is, it is all I have. You cannot be surprised, therefore, if I value and defend it.

The only acceptable reason for me to choose to change a previously successful behaviour is if it is no longer serving its purpose. If the reason for its no longer being effective may be laid at my door, I may feel threatened and will be defensive. If it may be blamed on you, I have an ideal way out. You change your behaviour and I will stick to mine.

To shake my complacency and have me consider that now may be the time to change my behaviour, your best bet is to identify circumstances or conditions which are neither within my control nor yours which would make a change now timely and effective.

Such neutral conditions might include:

● The actions and behaviours of other people:
  'Young people today seem to...'
  'Senior management are increasingly prone to...'
  'Women always...'
  'Men are such...'

● Characteristics of products or materials:
  'These modern materials tend to...'
  'The increasing use of salt on the road corrodes the underbody so that...'
  'Effects of metal fatigue do not show until...'

● Changes in the social, legal, economic or political environment:
  'With the mess that the economy is in today...'
  'The COSHH legislation means that we must...'
  'So much emphasis on "green" issues means...'
  'The government now seems to be hell bent on...'

CONDITIONS AND LOSSES

Neutral conditions

● New areas of knowledge or technology:
'What is now known about the effect of cigarette smoking on the unborn child during pregnancy...'
'Parallel processing means that...'
'Recent studies have suggested that intelligence is located in every body cell and so...'

The following are changed conditions on which I could 'blame' any adverse effects of continuing the behaviour I am seeking to change:

```
┌──────────────────────────────────────────────────┐
│                                                    │
│                                                    │
│                                                    │
│                                                    │
│                                                    │
└──────────────────────────────────────────────────┘
```

Neutrality check:

My listener could not blame them on me   OK ☐

My listener could not consider that I am blaming him or her for these conditions   OK ☐

The losses/problems that my listener is/will be experiencing are directly attributable to the conditions and not to any other cause
                                                      OK ☐

My listener will not feel that they ought already have taken action because of the conditions   OK ☐

If the answer to each of the above is positive you can safely build your case. If not, you need to consider whether you can think of more appropriate conditions.

BENEFITS

Although in presenting your idea it is essential that losses and potential losses which the listener may experience are presented as leading from the changed conditions in a logical chain, most people find that when they are planning their approach it is easier to consider *benefits* first. This is because the strongest potential losses are usually those which mirror the benefits of the desired behaviour.

People do not buy products, services or ideas, they buy benefits.

To win every time you need to know how to handle benefits to greatest effect. It is ironic that most salespeople don't, but when by happenstance they get it right the effect is magical.

If benefits are the key you need plenty of them. So record every benefit, no matter how trivial which the person you are seeking to influence will experience when you are successful.

Benefits of my idea, product or service:

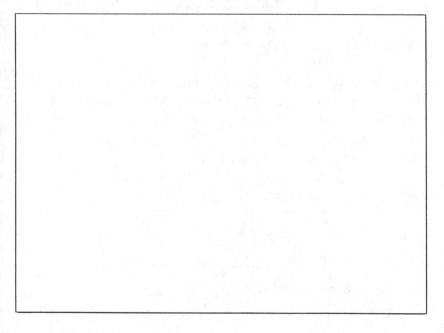

Go back over your benefits and exclude any *features* of your service, idea or product.

Benefits and features

Benefits are defined as the desirable outcomes which the user of your product, idea or service will experience in use. Benefits are the wonderful experiences, features are the 'technology' that makes the benefits possible. For example:

- 'Stunning sound quality' (benefit) from state of the art, elliptical speakers (feature)
- 'Luxurious comfort' (benefit) with our ergonomically designed seats (feature)
- 'Save money' (benefit) with our lowest ever prices (feature)

This is not to say that features are unimportant. They are the evidence that you can deliver the benefits, but the sequence is critical, and to talk of features as if they are benefits will confuse your listener and weaken, often irrepairably, the logic of your case.

The biggest benefit of all is the listener's most important goal which your idea can enable them to attain. To get them to say 'yes' you need to show an unbroken logical chain of benefits from your idea to the achievement of their goal.

Try to build such a chain. To make things easier and save you time, I suggest that you work backwards from the goal. (Hint for those unsure of what constitutes 'unbroken logic': only if you can in each case insert *which means* between the benefit and the goal and it makes sense is the logic established.)

My listener's key goal:

Benefit which leads to that goal:

Benefit which leads to the benefit above:

Other benefits in ascending logical order from my good idea:

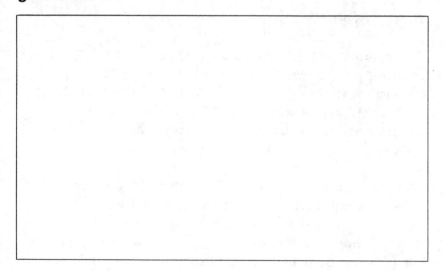

If you find that the logical chain is broken all that has happened is that you have omitted a benefit. Think about it and insert what is missing. If your idea or product will achieve the goal you will always be able to produce a logical chain although some of the 'lower' benefits may seem trivial. They are, however essential. Your ability to win every time is dependent on the other person believing the first and smallest, therefore most credible benefit, believing in turn that it guarantees the next and so on all the way to the attainment of their goal.

And there's more. By presenting a totally logical case you are massaging the other person's ego, or respecting their logical approach if you prefer.

Either way, it is essential to remember that we do not 'buy' anything, idea, product or service, for totally rational or totally emotional reasons. The skilled persuader uses both logic and emotion to achieve their goals and where it is possible to use both through a single proven process that is economical as well as effective.

Always think of benefits in the language in which you will express them. Language is far more important than those that have been seduced by the fantasies of 'body language' recognise. Be positive and personal at all times:

- Think 'you will…'
- Write 'you will…'
- Say 'you will…'

Forget about 'smart-alec' closing techniques. If you have convincingly, and that means logically, shown that using your product or idea will provide the benefits which you claim and enable the buyer to achieve a valued goal, closing techniques are unnecessary. If you have failed to make the case they are useless.

What then do you do with those benefits which your idea will deliver, but which do not fit into your natural logical flow?

You select one or two, no more, powerful ones to whet the listener's interest before you tell them *anything* about your idea. In effect, you use benefits which do not fit the logical flow to the achievement of the objective to sell the potential buyer on the idea of listening to you with 'favourable attention'.

As for the rest, you keep them in your armoury to prove the achievement of secondary objectives if necessary, or to enable you to deal effectively with objections if they arise.

If you have handled the sequence effectively:

- identifying and expressing the key listener goal as the target
- showing how changing conditions could or will lead to losses
- expressing desirable outcomes from using your idea

your buyer will want to know *all* about what you are offering. (And at this stage I do mean all. Consider the success of periodicals such as *What Car*, *What HiFi*, *Which?* and the rest of the consumer magazines. When someone is in the market the thirst for information is all but insatiable – and if you have said the right things in the right order, your listener is very definitely in the market.)

Analyse your offering to ensure that you are prepared to tell your eager listener all that they want to know to make the right decision.

- Think of the features. What they are, their characteristics and what they do. Consider especially how they create and sustain the great benefits which you offer.
- Consider the resources: those which your listener has which will enable them to get the best from your offering, and those which you can provide to support them in achieving their goals.
- Analyse the experiences of others who have used your idea or products. Be ready to talk about their success and the enormous benefits they have achieved.

Before offering references consider two things. High status users of your products are fine as long as:

- your present listener respects the users and their judgement
- the users you quote are not such 'big names' that your listener is automatically led to the conclusion that your product is 'out of my league'

You must have the specific permission of these users to quote their experience. You are neither breaching confidentiality nor simply name dropping.

If you are in the business of providing professional services, always be sure that when you tell your client the detail of *what* you can do for them, you do not slip into the trap of explaining *how* you will do it. You are in the business of selling your professional expertise. The *how* is what the client is paying for. Give that free and you are providing a recipe for them to do it themselves.

Remember the story of the engineer who charged £1000 for hitting a pipe with a hammer: 1p for the blow and £999.99 for knowing where to hit. What would he have been able to charge next time had he said: 'I just give it a firm tap here'?

Back for a while to your idea for changing another person's behaviour. Analyse your idea.

PRACTICE OPPORTUNITY

What will I/they do?

When will it be done?

Where will it be done?

Who specifically will do it?

What skills or knowledge will be needed?

How do the features 'prove' the benefits?

What resources are needed?

Are they available?   Yes ☐ No ☐

What support should I be ready to provide?

Can I provide it?   Yes ☐ No ☐

Who uses my idea?

```
┌──────────────────────────────────────────────────┐
│                                                    │
│                                                    │
│                                                    │
│                                                    │
│                                                    │
└──────────────────────────────────────────────────┘
```

Would they be happy if I quoted them?

Yes ❐ No ❐

Do they have appropriate status in the eyes of the potential buyer?

Yes ❐ No ❐

The *losses* which will be experienced by your listener if they fail to pursue your excellent idea or use your product or service will be to a major degree the mirror image of the benefits which your idea guarantees.

    For example: if a benefit of your idea was 'increased sales revenue' a loss might well be 'sales opportunities may be missed'.

If losses are tied to conditions rather than to the undesirable action of your listener, as explained above, you can be more direct and positive:

    'With things as they are right now you *will* miss sales opportunities.'

As the mirror image of benefits, losses must be logically linked to prove that unless your recommended action is taken the key goal or objective will surely not be realised.

Now we have the winning structure pretty well complete. The total logic goes like this:

LOSSES

- **LISTENER'S OBJECTIVE**
  You want *xxxxx* pretty badly

- **CONDITIONS**
  What you have done in the past has served you very well until now, but things are changing and you might be wise to consider how you should act to achieve your goal in today's different circumstances.

- **LOSSES DERIVED FROM THE CONDITIONS**
  The way things are going this is what will happen and you certainly won't achieve what you want when it does.

- **YOUR INTENTION TO HELP**
  To avoid problems and get what you want I have an idea or two that may help.

- **NON-LOGICAL BENEFITS TO SELL THE LISTENER THE IDEA OF LISTENING TO THE IDEA**
  You will achieve these major benefits if you...

- **THE DETAIL OF THE IDEA, SERVICE OR PRODUCT**
  Do this. You can do it because...
  Others who have done it say this about it...
  These powerful features ensure these benefits...

- **LOGICALLY LINKED BENEFITS PROVING THAT THE GOAL WILL BE ACHIEVED**
  And these benefits link absolutely logically so that if one is true all are true and you will get what you want. (Linking the first benefit to the appropriate feature is just the proof that is needed to start the chain. All subsequent benefits are linked logically to each other.)

- **PROGRESS TEST QUESTIONS** are used throughout the explanation of your idea to check the listener's understanding and acceptance of all that you say.

OBSTACLES

The skilled influencer welcomes obstacles or objections. They should be seen as indications that:

- Your listener is interested enough to want to know more about your idea or product.
- The relationship which you have built is robust enough not to be threatened by possible minor disagreement.
- There will be, as you answer the objection, an opportunity to get agreement and close the deal.

Research has classified the most common obstacles and our structured approach provides precise tools for handling each.

- 'It costs too much'
- 'It's too much effort'

THE PRICE OBSTACLE

This is best answered by showing additional *value*, and you do that by detailing some of the additional benefits which you thought of while planning, but didn't use in your logical proof that the goal would be achieved. That's why I ask you to be sure that you know *all* the benefits which your idea could deliver for this listener. You may not have to use them all, but it gives you great confidence if you know that you are well prepared should the need arise.

- 'We've always done it this way'

THE HABIT OBSTACLE

Answer this by reemphasising the conditions and the related losses that make now the time to forget about the old ways and consider a change.

- 'Smith's idea is better'

THE COMPETITION OBSTACLE

Concentrate on the *logic* of your idea. It does not simply offer benefits, it is a logically proven highway to success. If you can identify a unique selling proposition use it, but above all make the way you structure your idea and prove the viability of the desired outcome is what will make you stand out as different.

THE CONFIDENCE OBSTACLE

● 'We couldn't possibly manage all that"

Your detailed description of the features of your idea and the skills needed to put it into operation are the critical weapon in your armoury in dealing with this obstacle. And don't overlook the potency of an appeal to your listener's pride: 'As you know, Charlie Jones made a good attempt at it and he has relatively little experience when compared to you.'

Pride can be a powerful motivator. I remember during my General Motors days the story of two manufacturing superintendents, one of whom supervised the night shift and the other the day. As each shift finished the manager who had just completed his work would write in chalk the output achieved by his team that shift. His successor would read the number and his team would be expected to beat it. Output spiralled upwards and quality kept pace. The impossible became commonplace, and all because of two men's pride.

OTHER PROBLEMS

Sometimes, even in the best managed discussion, emotions become aroused for no obvious reason. Your listener may suddenly show signs of irritation or even anger at something which you have said. Such situations have to be managed.

The danger for most of us is that faced with something of a problem we are inclined to talk faster, and that does little good for two reasons.

● Your listener is no longer listening. They are thinking about whatever it is that has caused annoyance. Talking is literally a waste of breath.
● Trying to plough on means that you don't get a golden opportunity to bring out an objection, deal with it successfully and score at the very least some brownie points for sensitivity and awareness.

If the other person shows signs of being upset, don't speed up and don't confront them either as that may make them unduly uncomfortable. Do this instead:

- **Stop talking**
  Don't ask what's wrong. Don't look offended or upset. Just
  maintain a neutral but interested expression and wait. If you
  wait the other person will say something. It may not be what's
  bugging them but they will say something. When they do:
- **Listen actively**
  Listen, not to hear something which will give you an edge,
  but to understand exactly what they think and how they feel.
- **Reflect content and feeling**
  When you are sure that they have finished, and only then,
  paraphrase what seemed to you to be the key thought in
  what they said, or mention their feeling.
- **Show that you respect their right to think or feel as
  they please**
  Demonstrate empathy. This means tell them that it's
  perfectly OK to feel as they do, but be very careful not to
  confuse 'empathy' with 'sympathy'. Empathy says 'that's OK
  behaviour', but leaves you the option of correcting their
  thinking later. Sympathy closes all doors to you by saying
  'you're right to feel as you do.' If they're right and you admit it
  you may as well apologise for wasting their time and leave.
- **Handle the objection**
  When the emotional climate has cooled, and it will if you do
  nothing to stoke the fires, deal with the problem specifically.
  Never try to second guess an obstacle, in spite of what many
  sales trainers and books advise. You have been at some
  pains to show that you are listening. Any attempt on your part
  to ignore what you have been given and decide for yourself
  what the other person 'really' meant will destroy your
  credibility. If there is a hidden agenda it will emerge naturally
  from the listener if you handle what they say with care and
  concern.

Some expressions which indicate empathy include: *Empathy*

- 'I understand you feeling that way, many people do at first.'
- 'You have every right to be concerned until we prove what we
  can do.'

- 'That's a perfectly reasonable point of view. I felt that way myself until I was shown...'
- 'It does seem like a lot of money until we've worked out all of the savings. I'm not surprised that you were taken aback.'
- 'Others have expressed very similar worries. It's only when they see how it works that they feel totally confident.'

You will find it easy to guide people to the right decision if you structure the presentation of your ideas, products or services to satisfy their concerns in the order in which they arise. Figures A1 and A2 may help with your planning. They are designed so that the correct sequence of presentation is from left to right across the form, regardless of the order in which you prefer to plan.

NEUROLINGUISTIC PROGRAMMING

Neurolinguistic programming (NLP) is a relatively new science, but it has already shown itself to have enormous power to drive change.

The vital thing about NLP is that it is exceptionally economic in the time taken to achieve desirable outcomes. By understanding and applying proven techniques relationships are built almost instantaneously.

As always you need to apply two skills – sensitivity to others and flexibility in application.

John Grinder, one of the co-founders of NLP, says that there is one rule above all others in its application:

If something is not working, do something different.

To be a skilled and sensitive practitioner of NLP you need to commit yourself to the belief that you are not and will never be the kind of person who, when a door doesn't open when they push, pushes again, only harder! That attitude of increased effort applied to the same technique is the very opposite to what NLP is about.

To present an idea, product or service effectively to a prospective user requires two things:

BUILDING RAPPORT

- You must present your case logically, using emotional persuaders constructively in the right sequence.
- Your listener must listen with favourable attention to all that you have to say.

NLP can absolutely assure a state of favourable attention from the beginning by building exceptional rapport.

As a skilled influencer you must be or become an enthusiastic and accurate 'peoplewatcher'. Couples in love usually mirror each other's behaviour. As another example, if a woman picks up her baby and holds him or her to her breast, within minutes the baby's heart and breathing are in perfect synchronisation with that of the mother.

MIRRORING

These examples are a clue to what we need to take first from NLP.

People like to buy from those that they like, and most of all we like those who are most like us.

We all have complex approaches to thinking. Sometimes we think visually in still or moving pictures. Sometimes we think verbally by holding internal conversations. At other times we feel things either emotionally or physically in our minds. This last style of thinking is called 'kinaesthetic'. Although we are all capable of thinking in each style, one dominates.

THINKING SKILLS

Identify your dominant style:

My dominant thinking style is:

Verbal ☐

Visual ☐

Kinaesthetic ☐

WORK SHEET: PREPARING TO PRESENT AN IDEA

TO: _____

GAIN FAV. ATT.	OBJECTIVE What the listener wants	CONDITIONS/LOSSES What the listener is up against	BENEFITS Desirable results to the listener	ACTION What YOU want done	TARGET Listener behaviour YOU want to change	LOSSES Potential or actual problems listener faces
Mood & manner	ANALYSING: List as many as the listener makes you aware of.	Identify changing circumstances outside the control of either you or your listener which could cause the listener to experience losses and failure to achieve their objective.	Isolate one or two benefits which will not form part of your logical chain leading to the achievement of the listener's objective, and use them to introduce your good idea, product or service.	Express positively and specifically.	Describe positively – what is being done, not what is not being done.	Link losses logically to prove that the objective will not be achieved unless the behaviour changes.
Greeting	Screen to ensure that nothing in the list is something that your listener would not want discussed.	Link losses logically to the changed conditions and to each other to prove logically that, in the new conditions, the objective will not be achieved by habitual behaviours.	Write down all of the benefits whether or not they fit your logical flow.		If you choose to express what you want to see changed rather than relying on conditions, be careful to avoid confrontation – depersonalise where possible.	To avoid argument, state what may happen rather than what will – express losses in the conditional tense.
Rapport	Constantly ask yourself 'Why would they want that?' to elicit possible additional and longer-term objectives.	Be sure that your chosen conditions cannot cause the listener to become defensive.	Organise the logical flow of benefits from the features to achievement of the objective.	FEATURES of your idea:		
Questions	FOCUSING: Select from the list above the biggest single objective which your idea, product or service can satisfy.	Link to your 'give away benefits by expressing your ability to help: 'You can avoid this and...'	Retain the remaining benefits in mind to use when handling objections and obstacles.	What it is / How it works / Who is using it / What they say about it / Why your listener will be successful / Help and support you can provide / When action should be taken for optimal results		
Start your talk	Focus your presentation on that objective and its attainment.					
	Before committing yourself, check the listener's desire for this objective with a progress test question.					

Losses leading to FAILURE TO ACHIEVE OBJECTIVE

BUT

OBJECTIVE ACHIEVED

OBJECTIVE LOST

Figure A1

WORK SHEET: PREPARING TO PRESENT AN IDEA   TO: _____

GAIN FAV. ATT.	OBJECTIVE What the listener wants	CONDITIONS/LOSSES What the listener is up against	BENEFITS Desirable results to the listener	ACTION What YOU want done	TARGET Listener behaviour YOU want to change	LOSSES Potential or actual problems listener faces
Mood & manner	ANALYSING:					
Greeting						
Rapport				FEATURES of your idea:		
Questions						
Start your talk	FOCUSING:	Losses leading to FAILURE TO ACHIEVE OBJECTIVE BUT OBJECTIVE ACHIEVED				OBJECTIVE LOST

Figure A2

Think of someone you know really well.

_____ 's dominant thinking style is:

Verbal   ❏
Visual   ❏
Kinaesthetic   ❏

My evidence for this is:

```



```

If you want to know the thinking style being used by your listener, as you talk ask them a question, preferably one where they will need to think about the answer. As they think, watch their eyes.

● If they look up they are thinking *visually*.
● If they glance to the side, or down and to the right they are probably using a *verbal* thinking style.
● If they move their eyes downwards and to the left they are using a *kinaesthetic* style and sensing or feeling the answer.

Get them talking at some length and it will be easier still to make a judgement. People say very literally what they mean. So if I say 'I want to show you the whole picture' that is exactly what I mean, I have a picture in my head and I want you to see it too.

If I say instead 'I like what I'm hearing', take it that I really am indulging in an internal dialogue and what I have just told myself pleases me. Not only do you know that I am processing verbally, you also know that I am building your case in my mind. You are on to a winner... unless you blow it of course by ignoring my preference, and insisting on your own preferred jargon.

Similarly, 'this doesn't feel right' means just what it says. I'm thinking kinaesthetically and I don't like the vibes I'm getting. So take care to build my good feelings or you will fail to convince me.

Vocal style can give it away too. People thinking visually often talk fast. They have pictures flashing through their minds and they are forced to convey them to you in words. They have to be quick or lose all the shining, colourful detail.

People thinking verbally talk slower. They literally measure their words against the internal dialogue which is going on in their skulls. It is important to express things precisely and they will often pause silently to consider the exact word they need.

People thinking kinaesthetically tend to talk slowest of all. They pause frequently and they punctuate their thoughts with sighs and audible breaths.

Always talk the other person's language and you will have easy and interference-free communication. Get it together by vocalising to match their internal processing. Without exaggeration, sensitively tune your voice to their:

- pitch
- pace
- volume
- rhythm
- and above all tempo or speed of speech.

Do that and you have moved a long way toward guaranteed favourable attention to *anything* you care to propose.

As soon as you are adept at the technique of posture gesture modelling (described in the main text on page 55), you can start to add two more subtle skills to your repertoire.

PACING TECHNIQUES

It is vital to mirror behaviour, as I never tire of saying, with sensitivity and good taste. I separate out these two skills because they will require all your concentration if you are to avoid looking crass by doing them obviously. *Do not attempt them until the use of the simpler skills has become as unconscious as walking or breathing.* Only then can you be sure that you will be able to do them with sufficient accuracy and subtlety.

Head position

The first is an extension of posture gesture modelling. Concentrate your attention on the head of your listener. Hold your head very carefully at a similar angle as you speak. This is more difficult to do than you might suppose. Bad posture becomes so 'natural' to us that we tend to believe that we hold our heads much higher and straighter than we actually do. Most of us pull our heads much too far back and stick our chins too far forward for the good of the slim bones and muscles of our neck. Check your habitual posture frequently in reflective surfaces. If you don't know where you are starting from it is very difficult to know which way and how far to go. So until you are absolutely confident of your ability to mirror the angle and position of the head of another accurately, isolate and practise this skill.

When you are confident that you are able to cause the listener to move their head in concert with yours, you need to use your skill to make them more relaxed. The most relaxed position for the head, relieving all tension in the neck, is *forward and up* with the spine lengthened and the shoulders relaxed down and widened.

Now comes the mystery. If you attempt consciously to move your head to the position which I have described you will almost certainly create additional tension and stiffness. So the formula is not to try to move your head consciously at all. You must give a mental order to your unconscious mind and trust your mind to get it right.

To instruct your unconscious you do precisely what many of the best actors and dancers in the world do constantly to achieve a perfect and relaxed posture. You say to yourself:

● Let the neck be free
● Let the head go forward and up
● Let the spine be longer and the back wider

and do nothing but let your unconscious mind work on your body.

You will know when you have it right because the upper part of your body will feel light, free and relaxed. The lower part, from the waist down, will feel centred, grounded and very secure and stable. All aches and pains will vanish, and your energy and vitality will increase beyond the wildest dreams of snake-oil salesmen.

In terms of influencing your listener's posture your conscious role is equally neutral. Having accurately mirrored their head position until they move as you move instruct your subconscious and leave your body to do its work, speaking directly to their subconscious and through that to their posture and mood.

Once you are able to manage the gross head movements of others, the next stage is to model their facial expression and movements with particular attention to the eyebrows. As always mirror, pace and finally lead. When you can bring a look of interest and pleasure directly and unerringly to the face of another you are in business – almost!

There is one more skill to practise and learn and you will be a master communicator. It is not easy, but it is well within your capabilities, and it gives you benefits which you would hardly dream to be possible.

When you are fully adept at what we have covered so far and you are full of wonder, as you ought to be, at what you can achieve, begin to concentrate on the breathing of the other person.

Breathing

Learn to mirror the rate, the rhythm, the depth of the other's breathing while you automatically tune in to the more simple areas of speech, posture and gesture. This time, however, do not seek initially to impose a different and preferred breathing style on the other.

You could, very easily. This is a technique which is frequently used in hospitals to calm the overanxious or emotionally aroused, but resist the temptation.

Synchronise your breathing precisely to that of another and you will experience something a little strange and very exciting. When you are able to accurately reflect all elements of posture and gesture including breathing your body will adapt totally toward the other person. Your pulse will synchronise with theirs, the moisture of your skin, pupil size and muscle tension will all become a mirror image of theirs. You will begin to share directly in their experience, you will share their emotions (which are expressed in and which determine body posture) – in short you will reach the ultimate in empathy. You will truly have walked a mile in another's boots and you will know with absolute certainty exactly what you must do, what you must say and how you must say it to gain your goal.

NLP METAPROGRAMS

Metaprograms are detailed individual thinking styles which identify the most effective approach to easy and foolproof influence.

Approach versus retreat

Anything that you do, anything that I do we do to gain advantage or to avoid loss. But which?

Some people love to take risks, are motivated by winning and happily understand that to succeed in many areas you must be able to accept and learn from failures. These people are oriented toward *approach*. In seeking to persuade such people the emphasis needs to be very much on what is to be gained. If you talk to them about avoiding risk they feel a little affronted. In their world risk is the spice that adds flavour to the dish. When talking to someone categorised as being oriented toward approach, touch only lightly on the conditions which they face and the losses that they will experience. Talk rather of evolving opportunities and the new and exciting challenges which will lead to bigger and better benefits and the attainment of noble goals.

Others are *retreaters*. They are not excited or motivated by risk. The primary benefits which they seek are those which minimise or obviate risk. Ensure that the threat implied by the conditions which they face is perceived by them as severe unless they act and act now. Spell out the losses which are implicit in current conditions until they agree that they must act to protect themselves and all that they hold dear. Then assure and reassure them that you have the idea, product or service which offers total protection. Highlight features which minimise or obviate risk. Demonstrate that they will have your ongoing support and that others have successfully trodden this path before with your help. Ensure that they feel comfortable and safe in your hands before pushing them to a decision, but once a decision is made help them to take action quickly. When they take action do all that you can to accelerate the experience of benefits without pain so that the, to them, high risk of changing behaviour is copiously and quickly rewarded.

Internal versus external frames of reference

People whose attention is on *internal* frames of reference measure their gains by how good they feel about them inside. It matters little to them whether or not their triumph shows. What is important is their internal emotional state. The benefits most likely to persuade them will be those which are most congruent with their value systems, their preferred self-image or their comfort zones.

Those who are oriented toward *external* frames of reference seek benefits which are more tangible. Show them how to get a new BMW 700 series or a yacht, a fancy new office or a fancy new title and you will excite them. Talk to them of values or principles and they may well be impressed, but less likely to act.

Many of us, given an opportunity to take a new course of action, seek benefits which are specifically aimed at us personally. Others, perhaps more generously inclined, look first for the opportunity to do good for others.

Sorting by self versus sorting by others

Try to establish how your listener sorts potential benefits and focus on their needs. Make no value judgements – in influencing we deal with the world as it is initially so that we may change it in the longer run. If I appear selfish and egocentric, fine: show me benefits strictly for me personally. As I enjoy increasing personal welfare I may become more generous.

If I were to show you a piece of paper with a square and a circle inscribed on it and ask you to tell me your thoughts about both, would you be more likely to say:

Matchers versus mismatchers

● 'They are both plane geometrical figures with internal angles of 360 degrees...'

or would your initial response tend toward:

● 'They don't really have anything much in common. One has straight sides, the other is round. One has corners, the other hasn't...'

If the first way is how you view the world there are many like you. They and you are called in NLP jargon *'matchers'*. If you want to draw an analogy for such people, show them how things are similar and they will immediately grasp even complex concepts.

Assuming that the second response is more in your style, you too will have plenty of company among the *'mismatchers'*.

Research suggests that we are split as near to 50–50 as makes no appreciable difference. For mismatchers the opposite strategy is essential: if you want to economically and convincingly explain a new idea to them, show them how it differs from something that they are familiar with.

I have explained metaprograms in a little detail because they are important. To convince someone to take an action you need to gain and keep their favourable attention. You must be careful not to offend them by offering benefits in a way which suggests that you have made the wrong assumptions about them and their needs. You must equally make it as easy as you can for them to grasp what you are presenting.

Research in the field of human relations indicates that the worst breakdowns occur when people realise that someone who they thought was just like them turns out to have a mind of their own and opinions, ideas and values which are quite different. This is why the bitterest of hatreds often occur between those who were once in love. They feel betrayed when they discover that the person they believed in and trusted held different beliefs from those that they hold themselves. Not worse, simply different, but that difference has often proved enough to break up a loving relationship when strong emotions are in play.

Identify an important person in your life. It may be a customer or client, a prospect, a colleague, a boss or subordinate, a relative, friend or lover. Answer the following questions.

Do they:　　　　　　　　approach ☐　retreat ☐

In this, are they and I:　　different ☐　similar ☐

If we are different, what adjustments to my behaviour can I make to accommodate their needs?

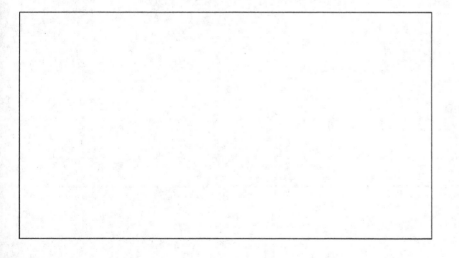

Their frame of reference is:　internal ☐　　external ☐

We are:　　　　　　　　different ☐　　similar ☐

If we are different, what adjustments to my behaviour can I make to accommodate their needs?

Do they sort by: self   ☐   others ☐

We are: different ☐   similar ☐

If we are different, what adjustments to my behaviour can I make to accommodate their needs?

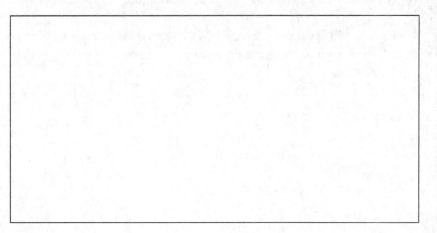

Are they: matchers   ☐ mismatchers ☐

We are: different ☐   similar   ☐

If we are different, what adjustments to my behaviour can I make to accommodate their needs?

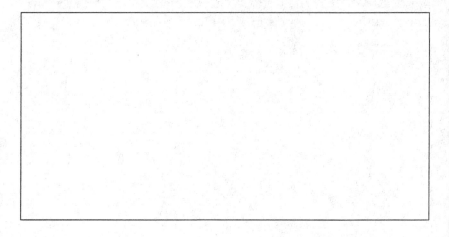

I have written much in this book about how to change the behaviour of others, but it is also appropriate to consider the possibility that to enjoy 100 per cent success it may be necessary to consider changes in one's own behaviour.

Much of what I have shared with you so far may be new to you and you are hopefully planning to acquire, practise and perfect these state-of-the-art skills.

To be convincing, behaviour must be consistent and congruent – so this is an ideal time to think about whether the new skills will fit comfortably with old behaviours.

For example if, like me, you are more naturally inclined to talk than to listen, you may choose to change that behaviour. If in the past you have read books, been convinced of the truth of what they say, but have failed to take action, that too may be something which you would like to change. Perhaps you would like to have more influence in the family, but you allow your 'workaholic' nature to keep you from them for long periods and you would like to get your drive to work non-stop under control. Some of us respond to stress by drinking or smoking to excess and we might feel that our chances of total success would be enhanced if we could kick the habit. Anything from failure to delegate to overeating: whatever you want to change, you can change. Here's a tested and proven step-by-step strategy.

Be specific about what you want to change *to*… rather than from.
  For example:

THE PSYCHOLOGY OF PERSONAL CHANGE

Be specific

- 'I will be a non-smoker' *not* 'I want to give up smoking'
  or:
- 'I will grow beautiful nails' *not* 'I want to stop biting my nails'
  or:
- 'I will be an effective listener' *not* 'I must talk less'

Write it down:

Painful results

List *all* the painful results for you if you continue the present behaviour. Write them all down. Associate *massive* pain with continuing the behaviour. If the list you come up with amounts to less than massive pain, go out and find some more.

Tony Robbins, a master salesman and a world authority on NLP, chose to become a vegetarian. Like so many of us who make that decision he liked meat. In fact he liked meat so much that anything else was only trimming. To his mind the meat was the meal. Yet he was convinced of the ethical and health case for a vegetarian diet. The trouble was, the way he liked meat he was more inclined to link massive pain to its immediate absence than to any long-term beneficial effect on his health or his peace of mind. He had decided and he didn't want to backslide, so he had to find a solution.

He arranged to visit a slaughterhouse. That did it. Eating meat in future would underline the contribution which he was making to the horrors which sickened him that day.

Maybe to give up smoking you will have to give voluntary help in a cancer ward. Whatever it takes, do it. You can stop any behaviour by linking enough pain to its continuance.

The pain I get from continuing to _____ is:

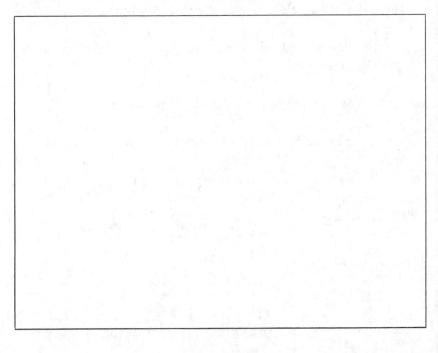

Massive pain will help you to stop a negative behaviour, but it won't put a suitable positive behaviour in its place. For that you need to associate the new behaviour with massive *pleasure*.

Pleasure

I will gain massive pleasure each time I:

Because:

Consciously seek out opportunities to interrupt the unwanted behaviour pattern by identifying times and places where it is most likely to occur and planning to stop it.

An opportunity to inhibit my no longer desired behaviour will be:

Inhibiting behaviours

Some people find that ways of inhibiting behaviours which they do not find useful are most effective if related to their dominant mode of thinking. Verbals prefer to give themselves a silent command when they find themselves in danger of slipping into the old behaviour, such as *stop* or *cancel*. Visuals may prefer to imagine a big red 'stop' button and to visualise themselves pressing it. Kinaesthetics may relive the feelings of an occasion when they successfully inhibited the behaviour and felt great about it. If you are a chronic worrier or subject to stress, try this. A simple technique can work wonders there too.

I will inhibit my no longer desired behaviour by:

```



```

I will recognise the need to initiate my inhibiting strategy when:

```



```

Rewards

Plan specifically to reward yourself for each and every success. Rewards may be a little treat or a simple self-administered pat on the back, or just giving yourself time to enjoy your triumph. The key is to reward *every* success with a small but valued reward rather than 'saving up' your rewards for something big at some time in the distant future. You can, of course, plan for the big reward too, but the small and frequent satisfactions have a more direct and powerful effect on reinforcing a desired behaviour.

> If you have a million dollars to give, better to give one dollar a million times than to wait until you see a million dollars worth of value.
> (B F Skinner)

Rewards which I can give myself from today include:

Design with care the new empowering behaviour and link to it rewards, both tangible and intangible. Be sure that your new behaviour creates its own satisfactions beyond the extrinsic rewards which you will add.

More specifically, my new behaviour will be:

These are the satisfactions which come automatically to me from performing in this way:

These are rewards that I now resolve to give myself in addition to reinforce my inevitable success:

Make sure that the new behaviour leaves no holes in your life. When I stopped smoking many years ago I gave myself an unexpected problem. As a smoker, having a cigarette had become an important reward in itself.

For example, if I were faced with a job which I disliked I would not smoke while I did it, instead I would promise myself a break and a cigarette after an hour of work.

When I stopped smoking I found it extremely difficult for a time to face up to jobs which I hated, because I could no longer look forward to a cigarette as a reward for effort.

Stopping smoking had given me many benefits. More money in my pocket, better health, a cleaner taste in my mouth and, most important, two children who were no longer worried at seeing their Dad apparently slowly committing suicide before their eyes. But I needed a new reward to fill the hole in my life which became apparent whenever I was faced with doing the accounts or decorating. A little yoga or a period of autogenic relaxation now fills that hole for me. You may need something to perform the same function.

Stopping this behaviour may leave a hole when I:

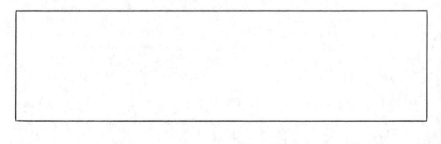

I will fill the hole(s) by:

```
┌─────────────────────────────────────────────────┐
│                                                   │
│                                                   │
│                                                   │
│                                                   │
│                                                   │
│                                                   │
└─────────────────────────────────────────────────┘
```

Finally, check that your new behaviour is ecologically sound.
That is, it damages no one and nothing you care about.

Many great scientists and thinkers have left writings which
indicate that they used similar approaches to solving difficult
problems. NLP research confirms that the approach which they
outline has the advantage of using the whole brain and
enhancing creativity.

NLP PROBLEM
SOLVING

While standard problem-solving techniques such as:

● Kepner Tregoe: for strictly rational problems of deviations
  from the norm
● Synectics: for problems requiring novel, attractive and
  feasible solution
● morphological analysis: to extend the life and application of
  products and ideas

are all extremely useful and should be in the repertoire of every
businessperson, this approach is most useful when it seems that
all others have failed.

The approach involves three steps.

● Specify the problem
● Involve the whole mind in the search for a solution
● Allow the subconscious to provide the answer

State in your own words as much detail about the problem as
will clarify it for you.

SPECIFY THE
PROBLEM

What exactly is the problem?

Why is it a problem to me personally?

Will it get worse if I do nothing?   Yes ☐ No ☐

Is it important ☐ or merely urgent ☐ or both ☐

Do I have an ideal solution in my mind?
Yes ☐ No ☐

If 'yes', write it down:

What, if anything, limits my power to act on any solution?

What additional information seems relevant at present?

What, if any additional information is likely to be essential to a solution?

Where can I get that information?

INVOLVE THE WHOLE MIND IN THE SEARCH FOR A SOLUTION

Brainstorm as many solutions as you can, and write every idea down no matter how crazy or old.

Make no judgements concerning feasibility: the only role at the moment is to involve your whole brain, right and left hemisphere, conscious and unconscious in the search for a solution. When appropriate as well as writing down ideas, draw them as little cartoons or diagrams.

My first 100 ideas:

Review your ideas, checking any promising solution against three criteria:

● creativity
● attractiveness
● feasibility.

Reject nothing, but if you have a solution *act on it*!

If no solution presents itself at this time and you feel that you have fully immersed yourself in the problem, hand it over to your unconscious.

● Stop thinking about it and put all papers concerning the problem out of sight.
● Formally hand the problem over to your unconscious by specifying when you must have a solution. Give your brain the maximum time appropriate to your need.
● Go and consciously do something unrelated to the problem.

This may seem an odd way to behave, but it has worked for minds as diverse as Einstein, Kerkule, Poincaré and Pasteur as well as Newton. Each of these great minds tended to favour sleep or a trance-like state for automatic problem solving.

In fact it has worked for you in a simpler form.

You forget the name of an actor or musician while watching television. It is on the tip of your tongue. You try unsuccessfully to remember and finally give up when frustrated by your failure or distracted by the programme. Minutes, hours, even days later the name pops unbidden into your mind for no apparent reason.

The next time that this happens to you try a little experiment. Consciously give up the search. Hand the problem over to your unconscious and specify a time by which you want the name. You may be pleasantly surprised by your brain's accurate timekeeping.

ANCHORING

One further technique of NLP is a valuable skill to the persuasion professional.

Imagine a situation where someone that you are seeking to influence gets excited and enthusiastic about your idea. They bubble with a desire to go out and do it, but you make the mistake which we all make from time to time. You oversell. Suddenly they are off the boil. You have inadvertently put other and less happy ideas into their heads. It would be good if you could easily and immediately return them to the previous state of delight, wouldn't it?

You can. All that you have to do is to learn the simple and subtle technique of anchoring. The keys to anchoring are:

● The intensity of the subject's state
● Acting at the peak of experience
● Accuracy of replication

We are all anchored to moods or emotions in our normal daily lives. There is no great mystery about it.

You may have had a situation where it was essential for you to get to an appointment on time. A great deal was depending on it and your car let you down. You had so set your heart on the outcome of the now lost opportunity that you vowed never again to own or drive a car of that make. That is a highly emotional response, but understandable. If, however, you find that whenever you see a car of that make, age and colour in the street thereafter you relive the pain, anger, frustration and disappointment of the earlier experience, that is anchoring.

Conversely, you may have met and fallen in love with the important other in your life by a dirty canal in an unpleasant industrial setting on a wet and windy day. You may then find that for the rest of your life dismal weather in a dreary setting inexplicably makes your heart leap with joy. Again, the experience of falling in love has anchored the tumultuous emotions to the most unlikely of settings.

To anchor someone, therefore, you need to recognise and act on the intensity of their state. There would be very little to be gained by anchoring a mild feeling of: 'Well, I've heard of worse ideas.'

But if the state is intense and there is major excitement and interest in your idea: then you anchor them.

So you have aroused an intense and positive emotional state, what next? You identify the peak of the experience and you act.

You act by creating a stimulus which, when repeated, will return the other to the peak experience you are witnessing. The stimulus may be a sound, a touch or anything which will be accurately replicable.

Those who are as old as I am may remember a radio programme with John Cleese which I believe was called *Listen to this Space*. There was an example of sound anchoring in an episode of that programme which worked beautifully. After a warm-up which got the audience laughing uproariously, Cleese introduced the word 'table' as one which had hitherto unplumbed comic resonances. From that point on any mention of 'table' brought forth hysterical and uncontrollable laughter.

You need a stimulus. Preferably a stimulus which is a little different from normal experience. If you frequently touch the other person, let us say on the arm, then an out-of-character touch on the knee would be appropriate. If your voice is normally low and well modulated, a little squeal of excitement may work.

Now comes the fun part. Once you have successfully anchored a mood it will come flooding back any time that the stimulus is accurately repeated. That is why there is a real danger to relationships if you catch the glance of your loved one when you are at the peak of an angry mood. Without either of you realising it, the repetition of that look will be enough to bring the bad feelings pouring back and before long you may start to think: 'I have only to look at him these days and I feel...'

Now that you have been warned you are innoculated against harm. You can use anchoring for all the best, most positive reasons: to return others to a state of enthusiasm and excitement, to bring back feelings of being unconditionally and completely loved. All the best feelings of life can be yours to give as a free and secret gift to others.

Anchoring is an important and life-enriching skill so let me repeat the key points:

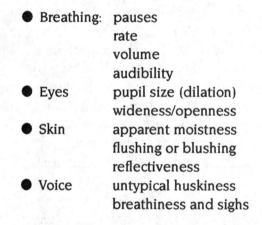

- The state to be anchored must be an intense one.
- Anchoring must be done at the peak of the experience.
- The chosen stimulus needs to be unique and acceptable in the context of the situation. It may appeal to any of the senses, but sound and touch are generally easiest to manage.
- To return the other person to the desired state, replication of the stimulus must be accurate.

To identify *peak experience*, look for changes in:

- Breathing: pauses
  rate
  volume
  audibility
- Eyes   pupil size (dilation)
  wideness/openness
- Skin   apparent moistness
  flushing or blushing
  reflectiveness
- Voice   untypical huskiness
  breathiness and sighs

This has been a brief and selective overview of the key ideas of NLP as they relate to influence. I strongly recommend all influencing professionals to buy or borrow one of the many excellent books on the subject of NLP.

MAKING THE FUTURE A LITTLE EASIER

To ensure the development of a constructive future relationship, the salesperson only needs to:

- ensure that what is promised is the least that is delivered
- continue to be actively concerned with the changing needs and expectations of the customer
- turn every customer into an ally by ensuring that they fully understand the value of referral business to the salesperson

An executive needs to do more. The range of factors which impinge on the relationship between leader and follower are subtle and complex.

- Domestic circumstances can cast a long shadow over the business situation.
- Relationships within the group can change rapidly and extremely, having a drastic effect on individual and team performance.
- An individual's confidence can run far ahead of competence or the reverse may be true.
- Illness can change levels of performance overnight. People's capacities and capabilities are greatly underestimated but highly variable.

The challenge of people management is that we operate with subtle skills on the shifting sands of human motivation and behaviour. The skills explained in this book are a proven methodology for success in this difficult and exciting area. Executives should, however, consider at least as carefully as salespeople how to maintain 'customer delight' after every 'sale'.

Start by ensuring that you clearly recognise the 'sale' when you see it and that each success is a firm foundation for easier 'sales' in the future. Where possible in influence situations have a goal which is:

- clear, unambiguous, worthwhile and meaningful to the employee as much as to the manager
- a reliable foundation for assessing the competence of the individual and the team now and hereafter
- consistent with the business's and the people's values
- sufficiently challenging to be a clear indicator of individual or team success
- inspirational enough to build enthusiasm and future commitment

Remember that rewards and sanctions are a major, and legitimate, source of executive power if used correctly. When influencing enhanced performance, use praise and reprimand, but be clear exactly what each will help you achieve.

When coaching for performance, always praise what you honestly can. It is a truism that even the most hardened individualist likes to be sincerely praised. Praising will:

- reinforce desired behaviours
- encourage and foster further improvements in individuals' performance level
- build confidence in tandem with growing competence
- redirect attention to the goals and their importance
- enable the praised individual to become a role model
- build the maturity of the individual and the team and enable to leader to accelerate the move to a more sophisticated leadership style

Combined with appropriate praise, essential reprimands have their own, and very different, purpose. Tony Robbins has said that the way to put an end to undesirable behaviour is to link that behaviour with 'massive psychological pain'. Reprimands are the element which creates 'pain'. The level of pain required to stop the undesired behaviour is a function of the degree to which the behaviour has been reinforced by past success; it does not need to be massive. Neither should reprimands be used in isolation. They can put an end to undesirable behaviour, but that is all they can do. That is why reprimands should, where possible, always be strongly laced with sincere praise. When they are they will:

- remind the individual or the group of the course to be followed and the importance of staying on course
- halt poor performance
- enable the leader to move back to a more controlling, task-oriented style on a temporary basis until behaviours and performance are back on line

If there were a law of reprimands it might read as follows:

Reprimands can stop people doing the wrong things; they can stop people doing the right things in the wrong way; they cannot, of themselves, ensure that people do the right things the right way – but this book tells you how you can.

I made the point at the beginning of this workbook that I cannot, sadly, hope to give personal coaching by telephone to every reader who would like to discuss their specific needs. On the other hand, if you feel that I can be helpful or if you wish to pass on concerns, complaints, comments or even compliments, then I would love to hear from you. I can be contacted at:

Beaumont Lambert International
51 Mill Lane
Greenfield
Bedfordshire
MK45 5DG
UK
Tel: (+44) (0)1525 713 503
Email: 100435.771@compuserve.com

A final thought from Ken Blanchard:

Leadership is not something you do to people; it is something that you do with people.

Bibliography

With the exception of the material which relates to NLP, little of what is contained in this book has appeared in print before. I cannot, therefore, provide a bibliography which will enable you to extend your understanding of the techniques outlined.

Instead, I offer a possibly idiosyncratic list of books which relate to social psychology, the general advantage which women have over men, the business world and the wider world in which business operates. What unites these books is their relevance, clarity and the pleasure which can be taken from reading any or all of them.

Abraham, R H and Shaw, C D, *Dynamics: The Geometry of Behaviour*, Ariel, 1984.
Argyle, Michael, *The Anatomy of Relationships*, Penguin, 1985.
Argyle, Michael, *Bodily Communication*, Routledge, 1993.
Argyle, Michael, *The Psychology of Interpersonal Behaviour*, Penguin, 1994.
Austin, J L, *How to Do Things with Words*, OUP, 1962.
Axelrod, Robert, *The Evolution of Cooperation*, Penguin, 1990.
Bandler, Richard, *Frogs into Princes*, Real People, 1979.
Bandler, Richard and Grinder, John, *The Structure of Magic* (2 vols), Science and Behaviour, 1975.

Bennis, Warren, *On Becoming a Leader*, Business Books, 1989.

Blanchard, Kenneth and Peale, Norman Vincent, *Power of Ethical Management*, Mandarin, 1990.

Burgess, Anthony, *A Mouthful of Air: Language and Languages Especially English*, Hutchinson, 1992.

Burrus, Daniel, *Technotrends*, HarperBusiness, 1993.

Cialdini, Robert B, *Influence*, Morrow, 1993.

Coward, Rosalind, *Our Treacherous Hearts: Why Men Get Their Own Way*, Faber, 1992.

Crainer, Stuart, *The Financial Times Handbook of Management*, Pitman, 1995.

Crawley, John, *Constructive Conflict Management*, Nicholas Brealey, 1992.

Engel, James F, Blackwell, Roger D, Miniard, Paul W, *Consumer Behaviour*, Dryden, 1990.

Erickson, Milton H (edited by Sydney Rosen), *My Voice Will Go With You: The Teaching Tales of Milton H Erickson*, Norton, 1982.

Farb, Peter, *Word Play*, Cape, 1974.

Furnham, Adrian and Gunter, Barry, *Business Watching*, ABRA, 1994.

Galbraith, John Kenneth, *The Anatomy of Power*, Hamilton, 1984.

Gardner, Howard, *Frames of Mind*, Heinemann, 1983.

Goldberg, Steven, *Why Men Rule*, Open Court, 1993.

Goldsmith, James, *The Trap*, Macmillan, 1994.

Grinder, John, *TranceFormations*, Real People, 1981.

Hamel, Gary and Prahalad, CK, *Competing for the Future*, Harvard, 1994.

Hersey, Paul, *Selling: A Behavioural Science Approach*, Prentice Hall, 1988.

Keyes, Daniel, *The Minds of Billy Milligan*, Bantam, 1981.

Koch, Richard, *The Financial Times Guide to Strategy*, Pitman, 1995.

Lambert, Tom, *High Income Consulting*, Nicholas Brealey, 1994.

Lambert, Tom, *Making Change Pay*, Technical Communications, 1995.

Lambert, Tom, *Key Management Solutions*, Pitman, 1995.

Leavitt, Harold J, *Managerial Psychology*, University of Chicago, 1978.

Mant, Alistair, *Leaders We Deserve*, Robertson, 1983.

McKenna, Eugene F, *Psychology in Business*, LEA, 1987.

Midgley, Mary, Women's Choices: *Philosophical Problems Facing Feminism*, Weidenfeld and Nicolson, 1983.

Midgley, Mary, *Beast and Man: The Roots of Human Nature*, Methuen, 1990.

Mole, John, *Mind Your Manners*, Nicholas Brealey, 1995.

Moore, Robert and Gillette, Douglas, *King, Warrior, Magician, Lover*, Harper, 1990.

Moore-Ede, Martin, *The Twenty Four Hour Society*, Piatkus, 1993.

Ostrander, Sheila, *Cosmic Memory*, Souvenir Press, 1992.

Popcorn, Faith, *The Popcorn Report*, Arrow, 1992.

Quek, Swee Lip, *Business Warfare*, Temple House, 1995.

Reed, Evelyn, *Sexism and Science*, Pathfinder, 1978.

Robbins, Anthony, *Unlimited Power*, Simon and Schuster, 1986.

Romaine, Suzanne, *Language in Society*, OUP, 1994.

Seligman, M E P and Garber, J, *Human Helplessness: Theory and Research*, New York Academic, 1980.

Sheldrake, Rupert, *The Rebirth of Nature*, Century, 1990.

Sun Tsu (translated by Thomas Cleary), *The Art of War*, Shambala, 1988.

Sutherland, Stuart, *Irrationality: The Enemy Within*, Penguin, 1994.

Suzuki, D T, *Essays in Zen Buddhism*, Hutchinson, 1985.

Tannen, Deborah, *You Just Don't Understand*, Virago, 1992.

Tannen, Daborah, *That's Not What I Meant: How Conversational Style Makes or Breaks Your Relations With Others*, Virago, 1992.

Tiger, Lionel, *Men in Groups*, Vintage, 1970.

Trompenaars, Fons, *Riding the Waves of Culture*, Nicholas Brealey, 1993.

Wilson, Edward O, *On Human Nature*, Harvard University Press, 1978.

Wilson, Edward O, *Sociobiology*, Harvard University Press, 1980.

Wrong, Dennis H, *Power: Its Forms, Bases and Uses*, Harper, 1980.